# 365

## SURPRISING
### AND INSPIRATIONAL

# ROCK

# STAR

## QUOTES

by ALISON TAYLOR
and RODNEY MILES

www.BiminiBooks.com

# 365 SURPRISING AND INSPIRATIONAL ROCK STAR QUOTES
## by ALISON TAYLOR and RODNEY MILES

First Edition

Published 2014 by Bimini Books

www.BiminiBooks.com

Cover Design by Todd Simpson

toddrsimpson@gmail.com

# Dedication

*For Brian Wilson, Jerry Garcia, Page McConnell, and Geddy Lee, who spoke to my soul and inspired me to become the music-lover I am today.*

—Alison

*To Elvis Presley, the first rock star I discovered in this life, and to Gene Simmons, who apparently wanted to be one and reached out and grabbed it. How many Halloweens did I dress as thee?*

—Rodney

# Now, Before You Get Pissed...

WAIT!

Let us start with a big, loud confession:

There are a LOT of stars and quotes we have missed! It's inevitable. We're sorry. There are so many, and if you love music like we do, you—as I would—probably feel slighted in some way that your favorite ROCK STAR might not be included.

So go ahead, get a bit muffed, but work with us—we have put heart and soul into this collection and we hope that will shine through, and hey, we had to stop someplace!

Another thing: verification. We didn't seek out all of these rock stars and push for written verification that they said these things, and we don't see that as necessary. Were this an academic thesis, of course we would have, but not in this case. Take for example, Gandhi:

*"Be the change you want to see in the world."*

That famous axiom rings well across the world—in fact it should ring even louder—but it's disputed that he actually ever said that. In fact, if we could ask Bapu (which means "Father") if he recalls ever saying that, there would at least be a chance he would not confirm or deny. Heck, Rodney swears his wife tells him things he said a few days ago that he hotly disputes!

So we are quite happy, for our purposes here, to have used, over this last year of developing the book, online sources of quotes that we find reliable enough. We don't claim to have found new, exclusive things these stars have said, nor did we include any song lyrics, but we do claim to have assembled these quotes in a novel, interesting, hopefully fascinating way, a way that hopefully makes them and the culmination of them new and enlightening or at least entertaining for you, dear reader!

So I hope you'll agree this collection is not complete. It's not perfect, but it's a damn good start, and I really hope you'll send me your suggestions, and even demands, for the next 365!

In fact, we have a similar tome with CEO/business quotes started! Sign up for announcements at www.BiminiBooks.com [shameless desire to connect with you!]

And *thank you* for buying this book! We sincerely hope it brings many hours, days, years of enjoyment and reflection. Read it however you like—a little at a time, one quote per day for an entire year, or even all at once. This collection belongs to you now. We hope you enjoy reading it as much as we enjoyed assembling it.

*What is a quote? A quote (cognate with quota) is a cut, a section, a slice of someone else's orange. You suck the slice, toss the rind, skate away. Part of what you enjoy in a documentary technique is the sense of banditry. To loot someone else's life or sentences and make off with a point of view, which is called "objective" because you can make anything into an object by treating it this way, is exciting and dangerous.*

—Anne Carson, *Decreation*

# Contents

# A Note From Alison

*Invisible airwaves crackle with life*
*Bright antennae bristle with the energy*
*Emotional feedback on a timeless wavelength*
*Bearing a gift beyond price—almost free*

—Rush, "The Spirit of Radio"

I BECAME A FAN at a very early age. The Beach Boys were my first love, followed by the cast of *Kids Incorporated*, followed by just about anyone who could weave poetry into a melody. No genre was off-limits. When I was a little kiddo, it was not uncommon to find me either singing and dancing in front of the TV (with a rockin' hairbrush mic of course) or trapped in my room with headphones blaring at an unsafe volume. I also sometimes recruited my friends to stage phenomenal lip-synching contests or to create mock music videos. Performance art was a way of life in my world, and most of my friends very willingly played along.

As I grew up, music is the one thing that remained constant. My tastes may have changed and refined over time (although I still adore The Beach Boys), but I have never stopped seeking out new music to listen to and share. Self-expression has never come easily to me, so I feel such relief whenever I find a song that mirrors how I'm feeling. After all, if someone has written a song about it, I'm obviously not the only one suffering through that particular trial.

For a long time, music was a fairly private thing for me. I either enjoyed it entirely alone or in the presence of one or two close friends. All hell broke loose, though, when my mom won tickets in a radio contest to an Oasis concert when I was 15. I couldn't say that I was an Oasis "fan" at the time, but I liked their music well enough. I was allowed to go to the show with a family friend, and I can honestly say that I felt my life changing during the two hours of that show.

Something about the sheer volume of the music combined with the lights and the energy of the crowd just spoke directly to my soul. It was as if a hole was being filled that I didn't even know was there. I wasn't allowed to stay for the whole show (stupid 10pm curfew that seemed totally unreasonable at the time), and I didn't even get to hear my favorite song of theirs. It didn't matter.

The bug bit me, and things have never been the same.

Over the years, I've latched on to quite a few different bands and the sheer joy of seeing them play live. When I was in high school, my parents didn't mind my fascination with concerts because they saw it as a very teenager-y thing. They even allowed me to take extended road trips with friends to see shows—sometimes for entire weekends. I was a good kid: I never did drugs (or anything else illegal) while at any of the shows. I simply got high on the experience and felt more and more fulfilled with every show. My parents truly believed the whole thing was a phase and that I would gradually grow out of it as I was faced with becoming adult and dealing with real-world responsibilities.

Well, spoiler alert: I never lost my unyielding love for music. In fact, it's stronger than ever. I spent a decade of my adult life battling a nasty illness that at its best was inconvenient and at its worst, completely disabling. People would always ask how I coped during the worst of it. The answer? A set of headphones and Rush's *Permanent Waves*. Or Led Zeppelin's *IV*. Or Phish's *Farmhouse*. Or Rage Against the Machine's *Evil Empire*. Or a homespun mix that somehow seamlessly transitioned from the Grateful Dead to David Bowie to Blink-182 to Taylor Swift. Music allows me to bypass the clutter and calamity in my head and instead have a direct conversation with my heart. It stirs up emotions that I could never imagine with my mind alone. Hope, pain, fear, joy: all are part of the musical experience, and all are part of the healing process.

On a more practical note, I understand that concerts have become criminally expensive. As a "responsible" adult, I know that I have to be careful and pay serious attention to what I can afford. Still, in many cases I'd rather eat ramen for a week if it means I get to check out of reality for a few hours and watch my favorite band do what they were born to do. It may not be the priority everyone would have, but it works for me and has for a long time. I lost count long ago, but I would estimate that I've seen somewhere between 200-300 concerts. Without a doubt, watching live music is my favorite activity.

It's hard for me to put my love for music into words. I often feel like they fall flat and fail to truly capture the weight of emotion I'm trying to convey. To many, I'm sure I'm just shooting words into the universe that are being received with a heavy dose of "so what?" That's the beauty of this book. For the first time, I don't feel the need to defend being a fan. Instead, I get to share some of the profound words said by the very people who keep me constantly coming back for more. The only real tragedy here was having to narrow it down so much.

May these words be uplifting, inspiring, and possibly even surprising. Most of all, may they help bring out your own inner Rock Star.

—Alison

# A Note From Rodney

*If you go down in the streets today, baby,*
*you better, you better open your eyes.*
*Folk down there really don't care, really don't*
*care, don't care, really don't*
*Which, which way the pressure lies.*

*So I've decided what I'm gonna do now.*

*So I'm packing my bags for the Misty*
*Mountains, where the spirits go now.*
*Over the hills where the spirits fly.*
*Ooh. I really don't know. I really don't know.*

—Led Zeppelin, "Misty Mountain Hop"

THIS BOOK IS NOT just another tool for toilet

breaks, seriously. We'd like to think of it as much

more than that. As Marty DiBergi says in his intro

to *This is Spinal Tap,* he was after something, but

he got more… much more. Well, so did we. As dumb luck would have it, by deciding as a labor of love project my writing partner, Alison, and I would specifically search out "surprising" and/or "inspirational" rock star quotes, we set a pretty cool standard. She got started on this thing and made a lot of headway before I really got into it and when I did I was very pleasantly surprised. The quotes were *surprising and often inspirational!* Duh! But isn't that true of all art—the idea is sexy enough but when you hear it played by the band or painted on a canvas, *wow!* Man, it feeds the soul in a way unlike any other I have found and it's right up there with raising kids or falling in love.

But let me back up for a minute. I was working on another book project, ghostwritten for someone else, and looking for some fitting and thought-provoking quotes to insert into his or her book when I played momentary hooky and Googled, "Gene Simmons quotes." There, I think it was on BrainyQuote or someplace, were all these soundbites on the situation in Israel. It led me to a YouTube video and other click-and-finds, and before I knew it, I was rapt by Gene's Semitism. But of course! Of course he'd feel that way! In fact, Gene's a very three-dimensional guy as far as I can tell. "The Demon" was not only a nice Jewish boy to a very large degree but he's a push-over family guy it seems as well; the guy who pioneered spitting blood, blowing fire, singing one and two-syllable songs about his penis, and being accused of being a Satanist! Here he was making more sense that *all* politicians on this foreign policy matter I had given ear time to.

It was surprising and inspirational, but then maybe I'm biased. After all, my own love affair with music started on a Winnie-the-Pooh record player my mom had gotten for my younger brother, Aaron, upon which I would spin her Elvis records, circa 1975 or so. I would set the thing up, raise the volume, drop the needle, and Aaron and I would jump back as the King blurted "You ain't nothin' but a hound dog..."

It was my first self-injection of the stimulant called rock and roll. I'm still a junkie today, thankfully.

Well, from there, a kid in my grade school, I'd heard, was into this band, *KISS.* "Eric, you're into

*KISS*?" I asked. He nodded as we were settling in to our wooden desks, I guess it was about fifth grade, Staten Island, NY. "And that guy spits blood and stuff?" Eric nodded again, but his eyes were alight this time—he *dug this,* I surmised. I was intrigued. I started with the *Alive* double album and the rest is history, really. I would don the demon garb on more than one Halloween and see them live I don't know how many times.

But as I grew, I grew out of the simplicity of the lyrics, for the most part. *Love Gun* is as painfully simple as it seems, which is reason to wince but then again, also a sort of sexual inhibition tester. Can you honestly, really, just set back and rock out to Foghat's *Slow Ride,* for example? I hope you can. When you're youngest these things are "cool" and edgy. As you mature these things are stupid. But as you age and the pretenses dissipate, they can be simple tests of your ability to savor the simple pleasures in life, and like a cigar, some fine wine, and perhaps a discussion of quantum mechanics or financial planning, each has its place.

And I had found a sympathetic soul in Alison. We were a budding writing team, having worked on a few books (ghostwritten and otherwise) together and we were launching a small publishing house, and I wanted to get up and running with a few really cool titles. We had just discussed music the night before via Skype (we've never met in person, yet she is one of my most valued friends and colleagues, a blessing of the digital age), and she had confessed "It's one of two things I'm really passionate about!" She then educated me on Primus and Les Claypool, who, I am a tad embarrassed to admit, I hadn't really heard of, despite being a Zappa fan from way back. So after I lost myself in Gene Simmons' surprising and somewhat inspirational treatises on where Obama had gone wrong, the synapses clicked and I asked her about doing a book of rock star quotes. She started that night.

I'd like to think the focus of this book, the criteria, has created more than some superficial "ha ha" statements found in songs or off the cuff before snorting some coke or grabbing groupies. In fact, for me, it's kind of a weird sensation: I found as I started to read over what we'd culled I was at once exposed to the third dimensions of who I previously took as simple caricatures. These guys were *people,* and many of them had some interesting things to say. John Bonham got nervous before "every show." Huh.

When we discover someone or something is not unlike us, well, it changes the landscape. Mankind is becoming less violent (believe it or not, but it's true) as the "circle expands" (to borrow loosely from a recent book title on the subject). So with these rock star quotes and the way Alison and I have approached them, I really think it's possible that a whole dimension of your own life (and which of us doesn't like rock and roll or has secretly dreamed of being a rock star?) might *unfold* right before your eyes as all of these guys and gals you might have taken as caricatures, just as I did to a large degree, become real. It's kind of fascinating.

Just be ready for various and unexpected themes. Cool diction and surprising views. Brains behind the bands. In fact, please, consider this a mosaic of thought, tossed together by us (albeit carefully) for your own interpretation. From what I understand, Donald Fagen usually refused to explain the meaning or inspiration behind most songs, e.g. "Haitian Divorce," and it was probably pretty savvy to practice such a discipline because even now all these years later, they're open to your own interpretation to a large degree (unless I simply missed the explanation of that song!). Then again, Jimmy Page allegedly said he had no idea what "Stairway to Heaven" was about because they were doing so many drugs at the time, and I'm almost glad (okay maybe actually glad) he can't recall, because for me it's a stirring and brilliant condemnation of cults or anything fleeting, like materialism. But it could be about any number of other things for you.

Good art *stirs* you. We can take completely different things from the same piece, be it a song, a poem, a painting, puffs of clouds, a flower, whatever. So do it, man, enjoy these quotes, and as Ozzy's friend Mr. Crowley would say, "Do what thou wilt" with them. That shall be the whole of the law.

— Rodney

# Rock Stars + Quotes

# Ace Frehley

*"ONE OF THE GREATEST gifts I've ever gotten*

*is my daughter."*

(1951-) Born Paul Daniel Frehley, Ace was the original lead guitarist for Kiss. He left the band in 1982 to pursue a solo career, but reunited with them from 1996-2002. He claims to have never been classically trained and has said that he does not know how to read music. Still, he is one of the most respected metal guitar players of all time.

*"WHEN YOU TAKE A shower in space, you have to press the water onto your body to clean yourself, and then you gotta vacuum it off."*

# Aimee Mann

*"THE KNOCK-OUT PUNCH is always the one*

*you never see coming."*

(1960-) Aimee rose to fame in the 1980s as

the bassist for the new wave band, Til Tuesday.

She has since created a respectable solo career for

herself, and has also appeared as a guest artist and

guest writer on others' albums. She has also been a guest star on several popular television shows, including *Buffy, the Vampire Slayer* and *Portlandia*.

# Alanis Morissette

*"I WISH PEOPLE COULD achieve what they think would bring them happiness in order for them to realize that that's not really what happiness is."*

(1974-) Originally a dance-pop artist, Alanis first made an international splash when she took her powerful voice in a more edgy direction. Her

24

third album, *Jagged Little Pill* became one of the best selling albums by a female artist of all time. Her mezzo-soprano vocals combined with her raw and sometimes scathing lyrics have helped her earn the nickname, "Queen of Alt-Rock."

# Alice Cooper

*"I'M VERY ROMANTIC, I'M extremely romantic.*

*I date my wife."*

(1948-) Born Vincent Damon Furnier, Alice Cooper has made a name for himself as one of the original "shock rock" artists. His dynamic music combined with his horror-themed live shows have earned him a loyal following and a successful career that has spanned five decades. His band was inducted into the Rock and Roll Hall of Fame in 2011.

*"IF YOU'RE LISTENING TO a rock star in order to get your information on who to vote for, you're a bigger moron than they are."*

# Amanda Palmer

*"TWITTER FASCINATES ME BECAUSE it's*

*real. It feels kind of unreal, but it makes very real*

*things happen."*

(1976-) Amanda is known for her unique and

dramatic stage presence. She is best known as the

lead singer, pianist, and lyricist/composer for the

Dresden Dolls, although she has worked on other projects as well, including a solo career. Her background is in theater, and she often brings theatrical elements into her musical performances. She is outspoken, opinionated, and no stranger to controversy.

*"I THINK I'VE BEEN addicted to openness since long before my rock career. I was terrible as a teenager. I used to go out of my way to make people uncomfortable with personal details. I was always fascinated by the idea that we have these weird, random boundaries between what we do and don't show."*

*"MEDITATION, ESPECIALLY FOR PEOPLE*

*who don't know very much about it and think it's*

*this very hippy dippy thing, can really be*

*powerful, terrifying even, as it lifts the rug up on*

*your subconscious and the dust comes flying*

*out."*

# Amy Lee

*"YOU CAN'T CONTROL ALL the crazy stuff that*

*happens to you. All you can control is the way*

*you handle it."*

(1981-) As the lead vocalist and pianist for Evanescence, Amy has become known for her operatic singing style and her goth-like clothing and accessories. She designs her own clothing, including her stage costumes and has always famously refused to conform to "traditional" standards of beauty and sex appeal typically present in the music industry.

*"WHAT URBAN OUTFITTERS HAS become is very much how I always dressed in high school by going to garage sales and getting stuff for 50 cents. Costs a little more now to look like crap."*

# Amy Winehouse

*"I FALL IN LOVE every day. Not with people,*

*but with situations."*

(1983-2011) Her vocal style was unmistakable. She combined soul, R & B, jazz, and reggae to create music reminiscent of another era. Amy's talent was extraordinary, and she was rewarded for it by being the first British female artist to win five Grammys. Sadly, she was a troubled soul and plagued by addiction and destructive relationships. She died of alcohol poisoning at the age of 27.

*"EVERY BAD SITUATION IS a blues song waiting to happen."*

# Angus Young

*"I'M SICK TO DEATH of people saying we've*

*made 11 albums that sound exactly the same. In*

*fact, we've made 12 albums that sound exactly the*

*same."*

(1955-) Angus formed the band AC/DC with

his older brother, Malcom, and remains the lead

guitarist. The band is one of the most beloved and

celebrated rock bands of all time, with their songs being played at every bar and party across the world. They were inducted into the Rock and Roll Hall of Fame in 2003.

*"WHEN I'M ON STAGE the savage in me is released. It's like going back to being a cave man. It takes me six hours to come down after a show."*

*"YES, WE'RE STILL FIVE little people with a*

*noisy attitude."*

# Ann Wilson

*"IT'S A REALLY BAD idea to be in a band and get involved with each other."*

(1950-) Ann and her sister, Nancy, are known for their work in the band Heart. Ann is the lead vocalist and main songwriter for the band, and is lauded today as one of the best female rock vocalists ever. Her powerful harmonies with her sister are iconic and inspirational to all women in the music industry. She also has proven herself as a talented collaborator and has had the opportunity to work with a multitude of artists over the years, including Cheap Trick, Alice in Chains, Elton John, Alison Krauss, and many more.

# Annie Lennox

*"DYING IS EASY. IT'S living that scares me to death."*

(1954-) Annie is best known as the voice of the Eurythmics, but also has had a very successful solo career. She has been quite commercially successful over the years, selling over 80 million records worldwide. She is also incredibly philanthropic and has done much work in Africa to help those affected by HIV/AIDS.

*"MAKING A CHRISTMAS ALBUM is looked upon by some people as the thing you do when you are heading towards retirement."*

# Aretha Franklin

*"AND I WAS BOOKED once to go on 'Ed*

*Sullivan' and I got bumped and ran out the back*

*door crying."*

(1942-) Raised as a gospel singer in her

father's church, Aretha embarked on her

commercial music career at the age of 18. She has had 88 charted singles, including 77 that were in the Hot 100. She has had more *Billboard* chart success than any other female artist in history. She was inducted into the Rock and Roll Hall of Fame in 1987 and has been called out by *Rolling Stone Magazine* as the 9th greatest artist of all time and the #1 greatest singer of all time.

# Axl Rose

*"I COULD BEAT MY mic stand into the stage,*

*but I was still in pain. Maybe fans liked it, but*

*sometimes people forget you're a person and*

*they're more into the entertainment value. It's*

*taken a long time to turn that around and give a strong show without it being a kamikaze show."*

(1962-) Born William Bruce Rose, Jr., Axl is the lead singer and only remaining original member of Guns n' Roses. His voice is unmistakable, and his stage presence is infectious. They are one of the most internationally successful rock bands in history, and they were inducted into the Rock and Roll Hall of Fame in 2012.

*"I LIKE TO BE real private; you don't always want everyone around you – even when they like you."*

# Barry Gibb

*"I HAVE A HUGE ego and a huge inferiority*

*complex at the same time."*

(1946-) Barry is known for his soaring falsetto, one of the primary distinguishing characteristics of the Bee Gees' music. He formed the band with his brothers, Robin and Maurice, and they have achieved incredible success over several decades. Barry is also a talented songwriter, not only writing songs for his own band, but for others as well. The Bee Gees were inducted into the Rock and Roll Hall of Fame in 1997.

# Beck

*"I THINK TRYING TO be offbeat is the most*

*boring thing possible."*

(1970-) Born Bek David Campbell, Beck is a master of combining and crossing genres to create something truly unique and striking. He plays multiple instruments and has an unusual vocal quality that distinguishes him from anyone else. He is a poster child for alternative rock, and his albums have achieved acclaim both from critics and fans. He is a four-time platinum artist.

# Bert McCracken

*"I THINK THE ONLY way to do anything powerful and positive with your life is to live your life with an open heart, and for us that's all that vulnerable means... The only way we can ever fall*

*in love or dare to dream is to allow ourselves to*

*be vulnerable. "*

(1982-) Bert is the lead singer of The Used. Turning against his Mormon upbringing, Bert experimented with drugs and alcohol as a teenager and young adult, eventually leading him down a road of addiction. He was able to pull himself out of it and has maintained stability since beginning his music career in his early twenties. The Used has toured extensively and has long been associated with festivals such as the Warped Tour. They released their sixth studio album in 2014.

# Beyoncé

*"ANY OTHER WOMAN WHO has to go to work and pick up the kids and make dinner – that's way harder than what I have to do."*

(1981-) Beyoncé's singing career began when she was just a child, as she entered into various music competitions. She eventually formed the girl group Destiny's Child, which is still one of the most successful girl groups to date. As the lead singer of the group, she developed her own sense of confidence and charisma and ended up striking out on her own. She has had meteoric success as a solo artist and is one of the most iconic female artists of our time.

*"I WANTED TO SELL a million records, and I sold a million records. I wanted to go platinum; I went platinum. I've been working non-stop since I was fifteen. I don't even know how to chill out."*

# Billie Joe Armstrong

*"MAKING MISTAKES IS A lot better than not*

*doing anything."*

(1972-) Billie Joe is the guitarist and lead vocalist for Green Day, which he and Mike Dirnt formed while they were still in high school. He has been writing songs since the age of five and always dreamed of becoming a professional musician. They hit remarkable commercial success with their 1994 album *Dookie*, and while their style is primarily pop-punk, they have branched out into other areas, even composing a rock opera in 2004.

# Billy Corgan

*"IF I HAVE RESISTANCE to something, it means*

*there's something wrong. The resistance to me is*

*a sign of fear."*

(1967-) As the lead singer, lyricist, and sole permanent member of the Smashing Pumpkins, Billy has created a niche within the alternative rock genre that combines elements of glam, goth, gloom, and pop. He is an outspoken advocate for mental health awareness, having suffered from depression, anxiety and obsessive-compulsive disorder himself. He also is highly spiritual and speaks often about spiritual topics, although he is not aligned with a specific religion.

*"COMPLIMENTS AND CRITICISM ARE all ultimately based on some form of projection."*

# Billy Gibbons

*"IT'S IMPORTANT TO COLLECT unusual*

*characters. It keeps you sharp."*

(1949-) Billy Gibbons and his band mate, Dusty Hill cannot be mistaken for anyone else with their signature sunglasses and long, full beards. Billy is the guitarist for ZZ Top and helped them create their blues-rock style. He is almost as well-known for his collaborations as he is for his work with his own band. Recently, he has appeared as a recurring character in the hit television show, *Bones*.

# Billy Joel

*"I REALLY WISH I was less of a thinking man*

*and more of a fool not afraid of rejection."*

(1949-) Raised by a classically trained pianist father, Billy became a pianist himself. He is known for being one of the most talented songwriters of all time, and also is one of the best-selling recording artists of all time. He has had dozens of hits over the years, but is probably best known for "Piano Man," which was responsible for jump-starting his career. He was inducted into the Rock and Roll Hall of Fame in 1999.

# Black Francis (Frank

# Black)

*"I'M AN UNTRAINED MUSICIAN. Untrained*

*musicians don't really have any music theory,*

*they don't have a lot of rules. We break the rules,*

*but it's mostly because we don't know what the*

*rules are. It's easy for us to go to certain places,*

*so I'm not surprised that a lot of people were*

*amused by my songwriting style."*

(1965-) Born Charles Michael Kittridge Thompson IV and probably better known by his stage name, Black Francis, Frank was the lead singer of The Pixies until their hiatus in 1993. He had a successful solo career for many years but has since reformed The Pixies and re-adopted his stage name. The Pixies are widely considered to be one of the most influential alternative bands ever created, and are frequently credited as an influence to iconic bands such as Radiohead, Nirvana, Weezer, and The Strokes.

# Bob Dylan

*"PEOPLE SELDOM DO WHAT they believe in.*

*They do what is convenient, then repent."*

(1941-) Arguably one of the most influential

singer-songwriters of all time, Bob came from a

folk background, eventually branching out to jazz, blues, rockabilly, and swing. His lyrics are generally focused on the counterculture movement of the 1960s, and his music became thematic of that time period.

He has sold over 100 million records, and was inducted into the Rock and Roll Hall of Fame in 1988.

*"BASICALLY YOU HAVE TO suppress your own ambitions in order to be who you need to be."*

# Bob Marley

*"HERB IS THE HEALING of a nation, alcohol is*

*the destruction."*

(1945-1981) Born and raised in Jamaica, Bob brought reggae to the masses. He began his career with his band called the Wailers, but eventually embarked on a solo career.

*"THE GREATNESS OF A man is not in how much wealth he acquires, but in his integrity and his ability to affect those around him positively."*

His music often included themes of spirituality, as he was a deeply committed Rastafarian. He died of metastatic melanoma at the age of 36. He was posthumously inducted into the Rock and Roll Hall of Fame in 1994.

*"TRUTH IS EVERYBODY IS going to hurt you:*

*you just gotta find the ones worth suffering for. "*

# Bono

*"OVERCOMING MY DAD TELLING me that I*

*could never amount to anything is what has made*

*me the megalomaniac that you see today."*

(1960-) Born Paul David Hewson, Bono is

best known as the lead singer of U2. He also is a

committed philanthropist, primarily focusing on

Project(RED) and the ONE Campaign, both of which he founded. They are both organizations that strive to assist ailing African populations. Bono writes most of the lyrics for U2's songs, and many of them focus on social and political themes. His soaring vocals are absolutely unmistakable.

# Brandon Flowers

*"WHEN MUSIC KILLS YOU, at least it doesn't*

*hurt."*

(1981-) Brandon is best known for being the lead singer for The Killers, but he also has released albums as a solo artist. He plays multiple instruments and wrote the lyrics to most of The Killers' songs, one of which won a Grammy award. He is an outspoken member of the Mormon Church and is featured in several of their promotional videos.

# Brian May

*"THERE IS NO WAY that you can ever really repeat something. I have this great belief that the magic of the moment can never be recaptured."*

(1947-) Brian is famous for being the lead guitarist for Queen. He wrote or co-wrote many of their songs, and has created original compositions of his own in recent years. His name often comes up in articles about the best guitarists of all time. He is also an acclaimed researcher in the field of astrophysics and was the chancellor of a university for six years.

# Brian Wilson

*"IF THERE'S NOT LOVE present, it's much, much harder to function. When there's love present, it's easier to deal with life."*

(1942-) As the founder, chief songwriter, co-lead singer, bassist, and arranger for The Beach

Boys, Brian has achieved international success and fame. He composed and wrote the album *Pet Sounds*, which is consistently regarded as one of the best albums of all time. His groundbreaking discoveries and techniques in the recording studio changed the trajectory of recorded music, and his influence can still be felt today. He was inducted, along with the Beach Boys, into the Rock and Roll Hall of Fame in 1988.

# Bruce Dickinson

*"MY DAD ALWAYS TOLD me, 'I don't care what you do. Just aim to be the best at it. Even if it's the world's best window cleaner.'"*

(1958-) Bruce is best known as the lead singer of Iron Maiden. He was not a founding member of the band, rather joining it in 1982, replacing Paul Di'Anno. Bruce struggled with the grueling touring schedule of the band and became burnt out very quickly when he wasn't receiving credit for his influence, especially in songwriting. He left Iron Maiden in 1993 to pursue a solo career, but returned to the band in 1999.

*"LIFE IS TOO SHORT to do the things you don't love doing."*

# Bruce Springsteen

*"THE PAST IS NEVER the past. It is always present. And you better reckon with it in your life and in your daily experience, or it will get you. It will get you really bad."*

(1949-) Also known as "The Boss," Bruce is a singer-songwriter who is best known for his work with his E Street Band. His songs often revolve around struggles in typical American life, which has made his music both relatable and commercially successful. He released a new album in 2014, and his band for the supporting tour includes Rage Against the Machine guitarist Tom Morello. Bruce was induced into the Rock and Roll Hall of Fame in 1999.

*"I THINK THAT YOUR entire life is a process of sorting out some of those early messages you got."*

# Bryan Adams

*"THERE'S NOT AN INSTRUCTION manual on how to deal with success, so you just have to rely on having great friends and a good team."*

(1959-) Bryan, known mostly as a singer-songwriter, is the best-selling Canadian musician of all time. He has also had an enormous amount of success during awards seasons: he has won 20

Juno awards in 56 nominations, and he has been nominated for a Grammy 15 different times. He is also committed to philanthropic causes, leading to his inductions into the Order of Canada and the Order of British Columbia.

# Bryan Ferry

*"I'M NOT REALLY SURE what it was, the best moment. You always hope it's to come."*

(1945-) Known mainly for being the lead singer for the art-rock band, Roxy Music, Bryan has had a long career that has been filled with commercial success. He has created three number one albums along with ten singles that cracked the top ten in the United Kingdom. He often writes his own work, but is also quite famous for his cover versions of classic songs.

# Buddy Holly

*"DEATH IS VERY OFTEN referred to as a good*

*career move."*

(1936-1959) An unquestionably influential musician, Buddy's life was tragically cut short in a plane crash following a gig. He was one of the first artists to write and perform his own material, and he is credited with creating the traditional "rock band" template: two guitarists, a drummer, and a bassist. His music combined elements from blues, rockabilly, and country, and paved the way for artists like The Beatles to take rock music to a new level.

# Buddy Nielsen

*"I HAVE FOUND THAT the people who are the most successful are the ones that always show up no matter what."*

(1984-) As the lead singer for the screamo/post-hardcore band, Senses Fail, Buddy has made a splash both in his recordings and in his live shows. His band has been a staple of various festivals, most notably, The Warped Tour, and they have created a loyal following. Their popularity has led to several of their songs being featured in the *Guitar Hero* video game franchise.

# Carlos Santana

*"YOUR WRINKLES EITHER SHOW that you're*

*nasty, cranky, and senile, or that you're always*

*smiling."*

(1947-) Known for fronting his eponymous

band, Santana, Carlos is one of the first Mexican-

American artists to achieve international acclaim.

He successfully fuses rock with Latin American

music, while adding other cultural elements, such as African percussion. His raw talent on the guitar ensures that he is frequently mentioned on lists of the "top guitarists of all time."

# Cat Power

*"I GOT MORE GUTS than brains, and that's my problem."*

(1972-) Born Charlyn Marshall and sometimes known as Chan Marshall, Cat Power is a singer-songwriter who has been a force to be reckoned with since the mid 1990's. She frequently collaborates with other artists, and has had the opportunity to work with big names like Eddie Vedder, Dave Grohl, and Yoko Ono. She also has worked on soundtracks for several movies, and has been involved both as a voiceover artist and actress for movies and television commercials.

# Chad Kroeger

*"SOMETIMES I WRITE ABOUT things that never happened to me that wind up happening to me. When you put things out in the universe, sometimes they wind up coming true."*

(1974-) Chad is known for being the lead singer and main songwriter for Canadian rock band, Nickelback. He is also a prolific producer, and has been part of a multitude of collaborations both on the performance side as well as the production side. He has been married to pop-punk star, Avril Lavigne, since 2013.

# Cher

*"UNTIL YOU'RE READY TO look foolish, you'll never have the possibility of being great."*

(1946-) Born Cherilyn Sarkisian, Cher is internationally known as an all-around entertainer. She sings, she dances, she acts, she does it all. She began as one-half of a duet, but has forged a dynamically successful solo career and has become a symbol for feminism and female autonomy.

*"I THINK THE LONGER I look good, the better gay men feel."*

She has starred on Broadway and in movies and is one of the best-selling artists of all time. She is one of few people in the world to have won an Academy Award, a Grammy, an Emmy, and multiple Golden Globes.

# Chester Bennington

*"YOU'RE CONSTANTLY TRYING TO prove*

*yourself, even after you've made it."*

(1976-) Known best for being the lead singer

of Linkin Park, Chester also created the band,

Dead Sunrise, as a side project. He is working as the lead singer for The Stone Temple Pilots as well. He reached enormous success with Linkin Park, particularly with their debut album, *Hybrid Theory*, which was certified Diamond by the RIAA in 2005. His name is frequently mentioned on lists of "best rock vocalists" and "best metal vocalists."

# Chris Cornell

*"TO A DEGREE, ROCK fans like to live*

*vicariously, and they like that, music fans in*

*general; but when indie music sort of came into*

*prominence in the early '90s, a lot of it was TV-*

*driven, too, where if you saw the first Nirvana*

*video, you're looking at three guys that look like*

*people you go to school with."*

(1964-) Chris began his career as the lead singer for Temple of the Dog, but is perhaps better known as the lead singer for both Soundgarden and Audioslave. His powerful vocals and four-octave range are unmistakable, and he is a talented songwriter as well. Chris has had the opportunity to participate in some exciting collaborations, most notably as the co-writer and performer of the song, "You Know My Name," which appears as the opener for the James Bond film, *Casino Royale*.

*"I'VE HAD A LONG career and I want to continue to have a long career. The way to do that is not to go away."*

# Chris Martin

*"I'VE NEVER BEEN COOL and I don't really care about being cool. It's just an awful lot of time and hair gel wasted."*

(1977-) Chris is the lead vocalist and pianist of Coldplay, and he has had a prolific solo career as well. With Coldplay, Chris has had the opportunity to participate in many philanthropic efforts and benefits and is an outspoken supporter of Amnesty International. He had a high-profile marriage to actress, Gwyneth Paltrow until their equally high-profile "conscious uncoupling" in 2014.

# Chrissie Hynde

*"IN MY EXPERIENCE LUST only ever leads to misery. All that suspicion and jealousy and anguish it unleashes. I don't want those things in my life."*

(1951-) Chrissie has ben a successful solo artist and is often cited as an influence for many female musicians. She is best known for her work as the lead singer of the Pretenders. She is a vegetarian and a staunch supporter of PETA and animal rights. She briefly entered the world of restaurant ownership when she opened the vegan-themed VegiTerranean in Akron, Ohio. The restaurant closed in 2011 as a result of the economic downturn. She released a solo album in 2014, which was her first new musical project in 35 years.

# Chuck Berry

*"IT'S AMAZING HOW MUCH you can learn if*

*your intentions are truly earnest."*

(1926-) Often considered to be one of the

pioneers of rock music, Chuck had a bit of a

rough beginning. After serving a sentence for armed robbery while he was still in high school, he straightened up his life, got married, and started playing music full-time. He is credited for creating the trademark "sound" of rock music, and was eventually one of the first musicians inducted into the Rock and Roll Hall of Fame during its opening in 1986. As of 2014, he was continuing to play live shows at the age of 86.

# Corey Taylor

*"THE FUTURE IS MEANT for those who are willing to let go of the worst parts of the past. When you cannot take two steps without turning around to inspect your footsteps, you are getting nowhere fast."*

(1973-) Corey is known for founding the band Stone Sour, but he is probably more famous as the lead singer and lyricist of Slipknot. He combines growling, screaming, shouting, and rapping with his singing, which has become his signature style. He wears a mask when he performs with Slipknot, just as all of the other band members do. He has collaborated on records for a multitude of other metal artists and is considered to be one of the most well-respected vocalists in his genre.

# Courtney Love

*"IN ROCK STARDOM, THERE'S an absolute*

*economic upside to self-destruction."*

(1964-) The lead singer of Hole, Courtney is
also known for her volatile marriage to the late
Kurt Cobain. She is considered to be a primary
influence for many female punk and hardcore

artists. In addition to her music career, she also has appeared in several movies and television shows. She claims that she never wanted to be a singer—that she would have rather been a skilled guitar player, but that she didn't have the patience to practice. She has said that she was the only one in her band who had the guts to sing. She has recently worked on some collaborations and has recorded several solo projects, but she is also reportedly in talks with the members of Hole and talking about the possibility of a reunion.

# Damon Albarn

*"I'M A WORKING MUSICIAN, so it's what I do.*

*I kind of always have lots of plates spinning, and*

*it's the ones that keep spinning the longest that I*

*end up doing."*

(1968-) One of the most creative minds in the industry, Damon is both the lead singer of Blur and the co-founder and principal songwriter of the virtual band, Gorillaz. He is a multi-instrumentalist and enjoys dabbling in a wide variety of genres, including rock, electronic, alternative, rap, and hip-hop. He is a supporter of the charity, Oxfam, and has performed as part of a supergroup in support of the cause.

# Dave Grohl

*"THAT'S ONE OF THE great things about music. You can sing a song to 85,000 people and they'll sing it back for 85,000 different reasons."*

(1969-) Dave is currently the lead singer of the Foo Fighters and was also the drummer for Nirvana. He achieved international superstardom after Nirvana's release of their album, *Nevermind*, but has forged his own very successful career since Nirvana split up. He is frequently asked to work as a session musician for other bands, and is highly regarded as not only an extreme musical talent, but also a positive and passionate individual. He has stated that as much as he loves fronting the Foo Fighters, he misses playing the drums, so he is always excited when he is asked to provide drum work for another artist.

# Dave Matthews

*"THE IDEA THAT WE'RE somehow centrally important to the planet's existence is pretty comical – although I'd like us to be."*

(1967-) Born in South Africa, Dave moved around a little bit as a child, but came to the United States permanently in 1986. He plays guitar and fronts his eponymous band. Between

2000 and 2010, his band sold more tickets and generated more profit than any other North American musical act. He generally prefers to play rhythm guitar rather than soloing, and he allows other instruments in his band, like the violin, to take the melodic front seat.

*"THE SADDEST PART OF the human race is that we're obsessed with this idea of 'us and them,' which is really a no-win situation, whether it's racial, cultural, religious, or political."*

~

*"MY SONGS ARE LIKE a three-legged dog — you have to get to know them to have any love for them."*

*"WHEN I LOOK AT how fortunate I've been,*

*being a musician... my response to being*

*overpaid is that I should pay it back to my*

*community in some way."*

# Dave Mustaine

*"MOVING ON IS A simple thing, what it leaves*

*behind is hard."*

(1961-) Dave first gained fame as the original guitarist for Metallica, although he was fired from the band in 1983 due to his issues with drugs and alcohol. He went on to become the lead singer of Megadeath. The band has gone through some turmoil, which has coincided with various ups and downs in Dave's life, including injury and religious awakening. In 2005, Megadeath founded and headlined an annual metal festival called Gigantour, which has been quite successful over the years.

# Dave Navarro

*"I'M AS OBSESSIVE WITH health as I was with*

*destruction."*

(1967-) Dave is one of the founding members and the lead guitarist of Jane's Addiction. He is also currently the host of the reality television show, *Ink Master*. He has talked openly about his mother's murder in 1983 and about how a viewer tip from *America's Most Wanted* was the catalyst that allowed police to bring the man responsible to justice. In addition to his work with Jane's Addiction, Dave also spent a brief period of time as the guitarist for the Red Hot Chili Peppers. He recorded one album with them before leaving due to creative differences.

# David Bowie

*"QUESTIONING MY SPIRITUAL LIFE has always been germane to what I was writing. Always. It's because I'm not quite an atheist and it worries me. There's that little bit that holds on: 'Well, I'm almost an atheist. Give me a couple of months.'"*

(1947-) Lauded as one of the true innovators in the world of rock and pop music, David's career has spanned four decades. He is a multi-instrumentalist but is probably best known for his unique voice and his ability to create themes and feelings with his music.

*"MUSIC ITSELF IS GOING to become like running water or electricity. So it's like, just take advantage of these last few years because none of this is ever going to happen again. You'd better be prepared for doing a lot of touring because that's really the only unique situation that's going to be left."*

He has always had a theatrical presence and even created an alter ego, Ziggy Stardust, who was extremely popular and iconic in the 1970s. He has also appeared in a number of movies, occasionally even playing himself. David was inducted into the Rock and Roll Hall of Fame in 1996.

*"ON THE OTHER HAND, what I like my music to do to me is awaken the ghosts inside of me. Not the demons, you understand, but the ghosts."*

# David Byrne

*"WITH MUSIC, YOU OFTEN don't have to translate it. It just affects you, and you don't know why."*

(1952-) David is best known as the principal songwriter and lead singer of the Talking Heads. He also has had a successful solo career. His most recent work has been in the theater world, as he has produced quite a few instrumental pieces for stage productions and ballets.

*"REAL BEAUTY KNOCKS YOU a little bit off kilter."*

He is an avid supporter of HIV/AIDS research and has lent his music to several compilation albums that were sold for charitable purposes. He does not own a car and can frequently be seen bicycling around New York City. The Talking

Heads were inducted into the Rock and Roll Hall of Fame in 2002.

*"SOMETIMES IT'S A FORM of love just to talk to someone that you have nothing in common with and still be fascinated by their presence."*

*"I WANTED TO BE a secret agent and an astronaut, preferably at the same time."*

# David Coverdale

*"I THINK WE HAVE two very important missions in life. One is to find out who we really are and the other one is to taste as much of life and experience as much of life as we can."*

(1951-) David began his professional career as the lead singer for Deep Purple, and eventually became the front man of Whitesnake. He transitioned away from Whitesnake following their boom in popularity from their self-titled album that included mega-hits like "Here I Go Again." He immediately began collaborating with various musicians. He worked with other rockers like Billy Idol and Jimmy Page, but he also branched out into other genres and even co-wrote a track with composer Hans Zimmer for the movie, *Days of Thunder*.

# David Gilmour

*"I THINK I COULD walk into any music shop anywhere and with a guitar off the rack, a couple of basic pedals and an amp I could sound just like me. There's no devices, customized or otherwise, that give me my sound."*

(1946-) David is an extremely talented multi-instrumentalist best known for being the lead guitarist and co-lead vocalist of Pink Floyd. While Pink Floyd was obviously a rock and roll powerhouse, David always felt like Roger Waters was in control of the band, and he felt like his talent was being underutilized.

*"USUALLY, IN THE STUDIO, on this sort of thing... you just go out and have a play over it, and see what comes, and it's usually - mostly - the first take that's the best one, and you find yourself repeating yourself thereafter."*

He began distancing himself from the band in 1978 to pursue a solo career, but then came back to take control of Pink Floyd after the departure of Roger Waters. It appears the two have put their feud mostly to rest, and David even joined his old band mate on stage in 2011 for a touching rendition of "Comfortably Numb."

*"IF PEOPLE WOULD LIKE to come to my concerts I'd love them to come. And if they like the music that I make, I love that too. But I do not make music for other people. I make it to please myself."*

# David Lee Roth

*"IT DOESN'T GET BETTER, it doesn't get*

*worse, but it sure gets different!"*

(1954-) Known as the original lead singer of Van Halen, David has also had a successful solo career and has worked as a radio and Internet personality as well. He was a creative driving force in the band, and was always a fan favorite.

*"IT'S ALWAYS IRRITATED ME that people say, 'Where's the action? Oh wow, there's no action here; let's go somewhere else.' These people will never find the action."*

He believed that Van Halen should be known for straight rock songs with lighthearted and fun lyrics, while guitarist Eddie Van Halen wanted more mainstream pop sounds and songs with deeper meanings. The differences eventually drove David from the band, although he reunited with them in 2007. He was inducted into the Rock and Roll Hall of Fame that year.

*"I USED TO JOG but the ice cubes kept falling out of my glass."*

# Debbie Harry

*"CAPOTE WROTE EVERY DAY. He said that's the only way, you have to sit down every day and do it."*

(1945-) Debbie has enjoyed a prolific career, both as the lead singer of Blondie and as an accomplished movie and television actress. As one of the original female punk artists, she earned herself a reputation as a fashion icon as well. Blondie split up due to a combination of business and personal reasons, but Debbie continued to be extremely involved with the music community, collaborating with many popular artists of the time. She also has made contributions to quite a few film scores, and she is a well-known philanthropist.

*"WE PROBABLY, AS PRIMITIVE people, made music before we actually had a language, and that's where language comes from."*

# Dee Snider

*"I WAS BORN AND raised a Christian, and I still*

*adhere to those principles."*

(1955-) Dee is known as the lead singer of

Twisted Sister. He came from humble beginnings,

getting his introduction to music in his church and school choirs. He is widely considered to be one of the best heavy metal singers of all time. He is also famous for his involvement in a court case that threatened to change the music industry. When the Parents Music Resource Center (PMRC) called for albums containing potentially offensive lyrics to be specifically labeled, Dee, along with John Denver and Frank Zappa, spoke out against censorship. The generic "Parental Advisory" label came out of this case, but the artists were successful in blocking the more specific label proposed by the PMRC.

# Derek Trucks

*"STARTING AT SUCH A young age in a musical family, fans will latch on to what you do and want you to stay there. You have to keep the flame lit yourself. That's what makes a musician great, the inability to box them in."*

(1979-) Derek was somewhat of a child prodigy on the guitar, landing his first paid gig at the age of eleven after only having played for two years. He has gone on to form his own band, The Derek Trucks Band, and eventually became a regular member of The Allman Brothers Band in 1999. He has had the privilege of playing with legends such as Buddy Guy, Eric Clapton, Stephen Stills, Bob Dylan, and Joe Walsh. He currently plays in a band that he formed with his wife, Susan Tedeschi.

# Don Henley

*"THE EAGLES ENDED ON a rather abrupt note, although in retrospect I realize now that it had been ending for quite some time."*

(1947-) Although he has had quite a bit of success as a solo artist, Don is more widely known as the drummer and lead singer of The Eagles. One of the most famous and celebrated rock bands of our time, The Eagles have sold over 120 million records, and they have won six Grammys. They suffered a high-profile and contentious breakup in 1980, but reunited in 1994 in a performance where fellow bandmate Glenn Frey famously said to the audience, "We never broke up; we just took a 14-year vacation." They were inducted into the Rock and Roll Hall of Fame in 1998.

*"SELLING EIGHT MILLION COPIES of your first album will mess you up."*

# Donald Fagen

*"I HAD TROUBLE DISTINGUISHING art from*

*life. I don't now, and I feel much better!"*

(1948-) Donald is best known as the

keyboardist and lead vocalist of Steely Dan.

While they started out as a traditional rock band,

all of the members except for the founding two

had either left or been fired by 1974. Donald and his original partner, Walter Becker, made Steely Dan their own personal project and ended up creating the band's most successful albums mostly on their own.

*"WHEN YOU GET A groove going, time flies."*

Throughout the years, they have both taken breaks from working together and have had successful solo careers. They were inducted into the Rock and Roll Hall of Fame in 2001.

# Eddie Van Halen

*"IF YOU WANT TO be a rock star or just be*

*famous, then run down the street naked, you'll*

*make the news or something. But if you want*

*music to be your livelihood, then play, play, play,*

*and play! And eventually, you'll get to where you want to be."*

(1955-) Born to a musical family in the Netherlands, Eddie moved to the United States at the age of seven. He is best known as the original lead guitarist for the band Van Halen, in which he and his brother, Alex, both take part. When the band started out, Eddie was the lead singer as well, but he eventually recruited David Lee Roth to take his place. He didn't enjoy singing, and since they were renting a P.A. system from David, they figured they would end up saving money if they let him into the band.

Van Halen has gone through lineup changes throughout the years, but Eddie's guitar style has always been legendary. He has his own star on the

Hollywood Walk of Fame as a result of his iconic

guitar work.

# Eddie Vedder

*"I DON'T NEED DRUGS to make my life*

*tragic."*

(1964-) Eddie began his rock career in the band Temple of the Dog along with fellow rock superstar Chris Cornell. However, he is best known as the lead singer and one of three guitarists in Pearl Jam.

*"I FEEL LIKE WE have to keep our eyes on the road. Being nostalgic is like taking an offramp and getting a sandwich – and then you get back on the highway. I don't want to be spending the rest of my life at the gas station."*

Despite Pearl Jam's huge success and influence on the grunge movement that had increased so much in popularity, Eddie absolutely hated being famous and is publicly known for staying out of the spotlight. He has dealt with stalkers in the past, and led his band in a boycott of Ticketmaster in the 1990s, preventing them from touring in the United States. He frequently collaborates with other musicians, often using pseudonyms.

*"I THINK celebrities suck."*

*"THE BEST REVENGE IS to live on and prove yourself."*

# Elvis Costello

*"MY ULTIMATE VOCATION IN life is to be an*

*irritant."*

(1954-) Born Declan Patrick MacManus, Elvis is a singer-songwriter who became a pioneer in the British punk scene of the 1970s. He and Paul McCartney are good friends and have collaborated on quite a few musical projects.

They also have participated together on ad campaigns promoting vegetarianism.

*"I USED TO BE disgusted; now I try to be amused."*

Elvis is a strong supporter of the tradition of jazz music and devotes much of his time and money to philanthropic causes that preserve the history and culture of jazz. He and his backing band, The Attractions, were inducted into the Rock and Roll Hall of Fame in 2003.

# Elvis Presley

*"I NEVER EXPECTED TO be anybody*

*important."*

(1935-1977) Known worldwide as "The King

of Rock and Roll" or simply just "The King,"

Elvis has made a permanent mark on the music industry. He started his career with country and blues tunes but gave them a more upbeat tempo, thereby bringing the genre of rockabilly into the mainstream.

*"TRUTH IS LIKE THE sun. You can shut it out for a time, but it ain't goin' away."*

His dancing and stage presence were revolutionary for the time, and while his act was exciting to young people, it made older generations nervous about music becoming a bad influence. He eventually went on to star in several movies and solidified his position as a pop culture icon. People may have been afraid of the changes he brought to music, but he is widely celebrated now as someone who singlehandedly moved a generation. He was awarded the Grammy Lifetime Achievement Award at the age of 36, just six years before his death.

# Elton John

*"I'VE ALWAYS WANTED TO smash a guitar over someone's head. You just can't do that with a piano."*

(1947-) Born Reginald Kenneth Dwight, Elton took his stage name in 1967, honoring two members of his band at that time, saxophonist Elton Dean and bandleader Long John Baldry. He may have started as the piano player of a blues band that was mainly a backing band for other artists, but he has become a living legend in his own right. He has sold over 300 million records, and is a prolific songwriter in addition to being a performer. He and his writing partner, Bernie Taupin, have worked together since 1967. He is an avid philanthropist and is particularly involved in causes related to HIV/AIDS fundraising and research.

# Eric Clapton

*"RISK IS TRYING TO control something you are*

*powerless over."*

(1945-) Eric has the unique distinction of

being the only artist to be a three-time inductee

into the Rock and Roll Hall of Fame: once as a solo artist, and then once each as a member of the Yardbirds and Cream.

*"THE TOUGHEST THING ABOUT being a celebrity, I suppose, is being polite when I don't want to be."*

He is widely considered to be one of the best guitarists of all time and has been influential to many rock artists. He is also a recovering addict and founded a rehabilitation facility on the island of Antigua to help substance abusers in need of recovery.

*"MY DEDICATION TO MY music has driven*

*everyone away. I've had girlfriends but I always*

*end up on my own. I don't particularly like it, but*

*I don't see a way 'round it."*

# Fiona Apple

*"I REALLY DON'T THINK anything I do is a mistake. It could be if I didn't learn from it."*

(1977-) A singer-songwriter known almost as much for her emotional displays as she is for her music, Fiona has had a long and largely successful career. She came from a creatively-inclined family and studied music as a child.

*"YOU KNOW, I'VE ALWAYS thought that it would be really funny if somebody made a romantic comedy where absolutely everything went well from beginning to end."*

She has a distinctive style that mixes elements of jazz and blues with alternative and rock, and her albums and performances have earned her eight Grammy nominations and one win.

*"EVERYBODY SEES ME AS this sullen and insecure little thing. Those are just the sides of me*

*that I feel it's necessary to show because no one*

*else seems to be showing them."*

# Florence Welch

*"I'M COMPLETELY IN LOVE with the world but also terrified of it. It creates some overwhelming feelings. Wanting to battle out that joy and fear is part of my music."*

(1986-) Florence is the lead singer of English indie rock band Florence + the Machine. Together, the band has released two full-length albums and is working on a third as of 2014. They have been nominated for three Grammy awards, including one for Best New Artist in 2009.

# Frank Zappa

*"ONE OF MY FAVORITE philosophical tenets is*

*that people will agree with you only if they*

*already agree with you. You do not change*

*people's minds."*

(1940-1993) Frank had a prolific career that

spawned 30 years and almost as many specialties.

In addition to being a talented musician, he was

also a songwriter, a composer, a director, a recording engineer, and a record producer.

*"IT ISN'T NECESSARY TO imagine the world ending in fire or ice; there are two other possibilities: one is paperwork and one is nostalgia."*

His primary interests were classical music and old-school rhythm & blues. As a result, his own music was extremely eclectic. He expressed his opinions about self-education and freedom of speech through his lyrics and was considered to be a huge political and social influence during his time. He was inducted into the Rock and Roll Hall of Fame in 1995.

*"THERE IS MORE STUPIDITY than hydrogen in the universe, and it has a longer shelf life."*

~

*"IF YOU WANT TO get laid, go to college. If you want an education, go to the library."*

~

*"I BELIEVE THAT PEOPLE have a right to decide their own destiny; people own themselves. I also believe that, in a democracy, government exists because (and only as long as) individual citizens give it a temporary license to exist – in exchange for a promise that it will behave itself. In a democracy you own the government – it doesn't own you. Along with this comes a responsibility to ensure that individual actions, in the pursuit of a personal destiny, do not threaten*

*the well-being of others while the pursuit is in progress."*

~

*"MY BEST ADVICE TO anyone who wants to raise a happy, mentally healthy child is: keep him or her as far away from a church as you can."*

*"THERE ARE MORE LOVE songs than anything else. If songs could make you do something, we'd all love one another."*

# Freddie Mercury

*"I WON'T BE A rock star; I will be a legend."*

(1946-1991) Born Farrokh Bulsara, Freddie was the lyricist and lead singer of Queen.

Freddie's powerful four-octave voice and gripping stage performances have led to him being categorized as one of the most talented musicians of modern times. His death of complications from AIDS brought new awareness to the disease and created an outpouring of support and publicity. Queen released 13 studio albums with Freddie as the lead singer, and they were inducted into the Rock and Roll Hall of Fame in 2001.

# Gavin Rossdale

*"I DON'T KNOW ANY musician who got to the*

*top without hard work. Take whoever you want.*

*They all work bloody hard, harder than you*

*think."*

(1965-) Gavin was the lead singer of post-

grunge band Bush, and has been a solo artist since

their breakup in 2002. His raspy vocal style, along with his stream-of-consciousness lyrics, were reminiscent of Kurt Cobain and Nirvana, although Bush did not have quite the same commercial success or impact. They were quite popular in the US after the release of their debut album, *Sixteen Stone*, but failed to achieve worldwide icon status like some of the other bands of the nineties. Gavin continues to produce music as a solo artist and in collaboration with others. He also went on to act in a few movies and married No Doubt's lead singer, Gwen Stefani.

# Geddy Lee

*"I PREFER TO THINK of myself as a musician who is still learning and trying to do something every time out."*

(1953-) Born Gary Lee Weinrib, Geddy is the lead vocalist, as well as the bassist and keyboardist for Canadian progressive rock band

Rush. His unusually high-pitched vocals and ability to multi-instrumentalize during live performances sets him apart from most musicians. All three members of Rush are widely considered to be at the top of their craft, and while they do not consider themselves to be commercial powerhouses or mainstream successes, they have an extremely loyal following. Their four-decade career is still going strong, as they continue to tour and release new material.

# Geezer Butler

*"WHEN YOU SEE ALL of these bands citing you*

*as influences, it makes you feel relevant."*

(1949-) Born Terrence Michael Joseph Butler, Geezer is the bassist and lyricist of Black Sabbath. He has been friends with Ozzy Ozbourne and Tommy Iommi since they were all teenagers, and they all played in various bands separately and together long before Black Sabbath was formed.

*"HOWEVER LONG THE SONG is was how long it took us to write it."*

Geezer is considered to be one of the most influential heavy metal bassists of all time. He was inducted into the Rock and Roll Hall of Fame with Black Sabbath in 2006.

# Gene Simmons

*"LIFE IS TOO SHORT to have anything but delusional notions about yourself."*

(1949-) Born Chaim Witz, Gene is the bassist and co-lead vocalist of KISS. He has also gained fame as a record producer, entrepreneur, actor, and television personality.

*"NEVER NEGOTIATE WITH kids. They don't have life experience, and they don't have repercussions for bad decisions; they still get fed and housed."*

His stage persona, "The Demon," along with his trademark makeup and wild stage antics has made him an icon not only in the music world, but also in the world of theatrical performance. He has never been one to shy away from controversy and has become the recipient of both great praise and criticism over the years as he loudly and publicly shares his opinions. Love him or hate him—his success with KISS cannot be denied. They have sold over 100 million albums worldwide and were finally inducted into the Rock and Roll Hall of Fame in 2014.

# George Harrison

*"YOU'VE GOT AS MANY lives as you like, and more, even ones you don't want."*

(1943-2001) George was the lead guitarist for the Beatles, and he also wrote some of their most well-known songs. After joining the band at only

15 years of age, George was often known as "the quiet Beatle," generally preferring to take guitar lessons and study during his downtime on tour. Later in life, he became enthralled with Eastern religions and traditions and eventually branched out into playing many non-traditional instruments such as sitar, swarmandal, and tambura. He also was part of the supergroup The Traveling Wilburys until Roy Orbison's death in 1988.

# Gerard Way

*"BEING HAPPY DOESN'T MEAN that everything is perfect. It means that you've decided to look beyond the imperfections."*

(1977-) Gerard was the lead singer of My Chemical Romance until their breakup in 2013. He is also a producer and a comic book writer. He has been public about his battles with addiction and depression, and has used songwriting as an outlet for recovery. My Chemical Romance was originally a product of social media's rise, first gaining fans via the social networking platform, MySpace. They eventually began opening for prominent bands such as Avenged Sevenfold, Green Day, Fall Out Boy, and the Alkaline Trio, which led to their huge boost in popularity.

# Gibby Haynes

*"WELL, SON, THE FUNNY thing about regret is*

*it's better to regret something you have done than*

*to regret something you haven't done."*

(1957-) Along with his college classmate, Paul Leary, Gibby formed the Butthole Surfers in 1981. Although they didn't see mainstream success until their single, "Pepper," in 1996, the Butthole Surfers were a staple in the underground music scene of the 1980s and early 1990s, attracting superstar fans like Kurt Cobain and Courtney Love. They are known for their unusual approach to music that often includes random noise, tape editing, sound manipulation, and disturbing displays of black comedy on stage.

# Glenn Tipton

*"IF YOU'RE NOT ENJOYING yourself, you*

*can't really look as if you are."*

(1947-) Glenn is the co-lead guitarist for Judas Priest. His playing has often been described as extremely technical and difficult to replicate. Judas Priest is considered to be one of the founding bands of modern heavy metal, and they owe much of their appeal and unique sound to the guitar "dialogue" between the two guitarists. Despite backlash against them for controversial lyrics and an accusation of inserting subliminal messages into their music, they are extremely influential to heavy metal artists today and have achieved musical and commercial success throughout their career.

# Grace Slick

*"WHEN YOU GET OLDER, it's not about what*

*you did that you regret, it's what you didn't do."*

(1939-) As one of the first female rock stars,

Grace influenced some of the greats such as

Stevie Nicks and Patti Smith. She was one of the lead singers of several bands, including The Great Society, Jefferson Airplane, Jefferson Starship, and then Starship. She also had a successful solo career following her departure from Starship. She had a very public battle with alcoholism, which has contributed to the content of her solo work. She has left the music industry and now channels her creativity through painting.

*"OLD PEOPLE SHOULD BE heard but not seen.*

*Young people should be seen, not heard."*

# Graham Coxon

*"I THINK A LOT of cynicism has dropped away*

*from my shoulders since I stopped drinking."*

(1969-) Graham was the lead guitarist for English band Blur, and has since had a critically-acclaimed solo career. He also founded and manages an independent record company, where he produces his own music and helps out other indie musicians. His visual artwork has become as recognizable as his music, and he specializes in album design both for himself and others.

# Greg Ginn

*"THERE AREN'T ENOUGH PEOPLE who are*

*scaring the kind of people who work at these*

*record companies."*

(1954-) Greg is known as the founder and leader of the hardcore punk band Black Flag. Many would argue that Black Flag was one of the first hardcore punk bands in existence, and they are credited for starting the punk movement of the 1980s. Although Henry Rollins was the front man for the band, Greg was the primary leadership presence, often bringing drive and discipline to the group. His diverse music tastes enabled them to bring punk to the next level, incorporating other styles into their music, while other punk bands had difficulty evolving.

*"THE SMALL COMPANIES WHO feel that the majors are a threat, or are predators, will use that as an excuse for their eventual downfall. Don't blame others for your own inadequacies."*

# Gwen Stefani

*"EVERY DAY I FAIL at something."*

(1969-) Gwen is a vocalist, guitarist, actress,

and fashion designer. She is most well known for

being the lead singer of ska-pop band No Doubt, as well as for her solo music career. In 2014, she also became a coach on the hit television show, *The Voice*.

*"AS A FAMOUS PERSON, you think how you're gonna end it, get away and have a normal life."*

She was invited to join No Doubt by her older brother, who was its original keyboardist, but she soon became the defining member, with her wild fashion sense and dynamic personality. No Doubt has sold over 33 million albums and they have received two Grammys in ten nominations.

# Hayley Williams

*"TO ANYONE WHO TOLD you you're no good;*

*they're no better."*

(1988-) Hayley is the lead singer of Paramore. She was initially discovered by Atlantic records while she was working with Nashville songwriters as a teenager. They wanted to promote her as a solo artist, but she was determined to front a pop-punk band. They allowed her to form a band with a few of her friends, and with the record company's help, Paramore has become a huge success. Hayley also is a fashion icon and recently released her own makeup line with MAC Cosmetics.

# Henry Rollins

*"SCAR TISSUE IS STRONGER than regular tissue. Realize the strength, move on."*

(1961-) Henry gained fame as the lead singer for the hardcore punk band Black Flag, but he has become better known more recently as a music journalist, actor, spoken word artist, activist, and radio host. During his time with Black Flag, he made a heavy impression on fans and critics, as his performances were raw, emotional, and animalistic. Eventually, his stage persona became disturbing even for his fellow band members. After Black Flag's disbanding, he dabbled in solo projects for a little while before turning his primary focus away from music.

# Herbie Hancock

*"I HAVE TO BE careful not to let the world*

*dazzle me so much that I forget I'm a husband*

*and a father."*

(1940-) Herbie is a jazz pianist, composer, and bandleader who has embraced many other styles as well, including funk, blues, and even elements of classical. He was called a child prodigy due to his innate skill on the piano, and he taught himself jazz techniques based on bands he liked to listen to as a kid. He has collaborated with many artists over the years in addition to touring internationally with his own band.

*"THE TRUTH IS THAT everyone is somebody already."*

He has released 41 studio albums as well as numerous live albums, soundtracks, singles, and compilation albums. Herbie has also won 14 Grammy awards.

*"TAKE WHATEVER HAPPENS AND try to make it work."*

# Iggy Pop

*"WHEN THE 'GODFATHER OF punk' thing*

*started floatin' around, it was, I was really, really*

*embarrassed. I thought I should have a great, big*

*rig and a cape and everything, and it was very*

*embarrassing. And then after a while, you learn*

*that if people call you anything, this is a great*

*gift."*

(1947-) Born James Newell Osterberg Jr., Iggy is the lead singer of The Stooges. He was heavily influenced by Jim Morrison's performances with The Doors, and he has modeled his own stage persona after Jim's.

*"WHAT DID CHRIST REALLY do? He hung out with hard-drinking fishermen."*

Fans have been known to show up at Stooges shows just to see what kind of outrageous stunt Iggy will pull. He is the first musician ever known to stage-dive.

*"SECOND ONLY TO THE sea, the Miami sky has been the greatest comfort in my life past 50. On a good day, when the wind blows from the south, the light here is diffuse and forgiving."*

He struggled with addiction early in his career leading to tension in the band, but they managed to prevail through several breakups. The Stooges were inducted into the Rock and Roll Hall of Fame in 2010.

*"I FIND IT HARD to focus looking forward. So I look backward."*

# Imogen Heap

*"I'LL MEET SOMEONE ON the street and blurt*

*out my most intimate details. I think everybody*

*secretly – or not so secretly – wants to be*

*understood, and I just want to connect, you*

*know?"*

(1977-) Imogen was one-half of the electronic pop duo Frou Frou, and she has also had a prolific career as a solo artist and record producer. She was musically inclined as a child and took lessons on several classical instruments for a short time, but she has been primarily self-taught. She has had a big presence on social media and has used various platforms to promote her music and communicate with her fans. She has won one Grammy award out of four nominations.

# Ivan Moody

*"SO YEAH, I STILL vomit before every show, slap the shit out of myself and just make sure that whatever I have to do to get myself in the state of mind that I need to be in to get up there, I do it."*

(1980-) Also known by his stage name, Ghost, Ivan is the lead singer for Five Finger Death Punch. They have received much praise for being such a promising young act in the heavy metal genre, and their record sales have reflected this. They have released five studio albums and have spent tremendous time touring, both on the rock festival circuit and on their own.

# Jack Black

*"THE MOVIE* SPINAL TAP *ruled my world. It's*

*for rock what* The Sound of Music *was for the*

*hills. They really nailed how dumb rock can be."*

(1969-) Best known as a comedic actor, Jack is also a talented musician and one-half of the duo Tenacious D. Their style fuses comedy with rock, and Jack's theatrical vocal style has led many to categorize their songs as "comedic rock opera."

*"I'VE HAD SO MANY hot, cheesy, corny loves of music in my life. I had a very intense Billy Joel period. So once you've Joeled it up – there's some good periods of Joel; it's not all hot cheese. But I can't judge anyone else for their cheese. I've deep-sea dived in the Gouda."*

Their popularity started with an eponymous television show, but their success encouraged them to keep creating music and tour as an act unto themselves. They have released three studio albums and have made many guest appearances in movies, television shows, and other artists' music videos.

# Jack White

*"IF YOU DON'T HAVE a struggle already inside you or around you, you have to make one up."*

(1975) Born John Anthony Gillis, Jack is best known for being the guitarist and primary songwriter for The White Stripes, a rock duo he formed with his then-wife. Together, they released six studio albums, three of which have won Grammy awards. Their style combined elements of blues, rock, folk, punk, and country. They believed in a minimalist approach to performing and recording. Following their breakup, Jack also has played with The Raconteurs, The Dead Weather, and as a solo artist.

# Jaco Pastorius

*"MUSIC IS IN THE air. It's my job to pull it out."*

(1951-1987) Jaco was an electronic bass player and bandleader, who more or less revolutionized bass playing for modern artists like Geddy Lee, Les Claypool, and Flea. His style was primarily rooted in jazz, but he added elements of Latin and funk to create an entirely new experience.

*"WHY A MANAGER? I don't need to pay anyone to say how great I am."*

He was always praised for his highly technical work, especially with a fretless bass and with harmonies. He was known mostly for his solo work and his work with Joni Mitchell. His untimely death at the age of 35 was a big loss for the music industry.

*"THE SECRET TO THE sound is to drop the bass on the floor!"*

# James Brown

*"I USED TO THINK like Moses. That knocked*

*me down for a couple years and put me in prison.*

*Then I start thinking like Job. Job waited and*

*became the wealthiest and richest man ever*

*'cause he believed in God."*

(1933-2006) Known to many as "The

Godfather of Soul," James had a successful career

that spanned six decades. He started as a gospel singer, but was quickly recognized as an incredible live performer with a passion for rhythm & blues.

He was part of many bands before eventually becoming a bandleader himself and creating a more "Africanized" style of R & B. This is what became funk as we know it today. He had a reputation for lengthy and energetic live shows that always brought the house down and left the audience as exhausted as they left him. He was one of the first inductees into the Rock and Roll Hall of Fame in 1986, and he had 41 singles that made the Billboard Top 100 chart.

# James Hetfield

*"AS FAR AS ARTISTS and musicians, they don't retire. They might tour less."*

(1963-) James is the songwriter and lead singer for Metallica. He also plays rhythm guitar for the group, although he has been known to take lead and solo from time to time, which has earned him high accolades as a heavy metal guitarist.

*"IT'S ALL FUN AND games till someone loses an eye, then it's just fun you can't see."*

Formed in 1981, Metallica was one of the first thrash metal bands to achieve mainstream success. They have won nine Grammy awards and were inducted into the Rock and Roll Hall of Fame in 2009. James and drummer Lars Ulrich are the only two remaining original members of the band, but their leadership has ensured the band's continuing success despite multiple lineup changes.

# Janis Joplin

*"ON STAGE I MAKE love to twenty five*

*thousand people; and then I go home alone."*

(1943-1970) Janis was a folk and blues singer-songwriter who gained fame during the late 1960s. She performed as a part of several bands, but her most well-known songs were part of her career as a solo artist. She performed at several monumental events, including Woodstock in 1969. She is known as the "Queen of Psychadelic Soul," and despite her obvious talent and promising future in the music industry, she struggled with addiction, which eventually took her life at the age of 27. She was inducted into the Rock and Roll Hall of Fame in 1995.

# Jared Leto

*"DREAM AS BIG AS you want to. It's the*

*cheapest thing you'll ever do."*

(1971-) Jared is the founder and lead singer of
30 Seconds to Mars. He is also an accomplished
actor, having played several critically acclaimed
roles. Success for 30 Seconds to Mars started off

slowly with their music gaining a cult following but not much mainstream success. Their second album, however, received radio airplay and eventually went platinum in the US. In 2008, the band was part of a high-profile lawsuit against their former record company, which spawned much of the creative material for their third album, *This is War*, as well as a documentary about the legal battle.

Jared and his band members are also activists for environmental causes.

# Jay Kay

*"THE MID-LIFE CRISIS is just those times when you're not so into the things were when you were younger."*

(1969-) Born Jason Luis Cheetham, Jay is the lead singer of Jamiroquai. Their style is best described as "funk + acid jazz," and they helped make this style of music become popular in the

UK. They have toured extensively across the world, and they have sold over 40 million albums worldwide. They won a Grammy award in 1998 for their mega-hit, "Virtual Insanity." Jay is also a television personality and races cars in his spare time.

*"I LEARN FAST AND I take note of what I've been told."*

# Jeff Beck

*"MY FIRST WIFE SAID, 'It's either that guitar or me,' you know – and I give you three guesses which one went."*

(1944-) Jeff is well-respected in the music industry as one of the greatest guitarists out there, despite not having as much fame or commercial success as many of his peers. He was part of The

Yardbirds after Eric Clapton left, but the majority of this career has been as a solo artist. His style incorporates elements of blues, jazz, heavy metal, and electronica, and his diverse tastes have made him the perfect collaboration partner for a variety of artists over the years. He was inducted into the Rock and Roll Hall of Fame two times—once with The Yardbirds in 1992 and then again as a solo artist in 2009.

# Jeff Buckley

*"I WANT TO BE ripped apart by music. I want it to be something that feeds and replenishes, or that totally sucks the life out of you. I want to be dashed against the rocks."*

(1966-1997) Widely considered to be one of the greatest singers of all time, most of Jeff's commercial success came after his untimely drowning death at the age of 30. He struggled to break into the music industry, often singing backing vocals for various bands and rarely staying with any one group for long. His breakthrough came when he sang at a tribute concert for his father, the late Tim Buckley, and his gripping vocal performance gained him attention from producers and record executives. He only recorded one studio album, having died in the process of working on his second. Many bootlegs of live performances can be found and are coveted by record collectors.

# Jello Biafra

*"FOR EVERY PROHIBITION YOU create, you*

*also create an underground."*

(1958-) Born Eric Reed Boucher, Jello is best

known as the former lead singer for punk band

Dead Kennedys. The Dead Kennedys were a huge

part of the hardcore punk scene in the 1980s that

also included huge names like Black Flag and the Circle Jerks.

*"PUNK IS NOT DEAD. Punk will only die when corporations can exploit and mass produce it."*

Jello's lyrics are famous for being harsh and politically charged, much in the style of Frank Zappa. After leaving the band over royalty disputes, Jello became a spoken word artist and a political activist. He ran against Ralph Nader for the 2000 Presidential nomination for the Green Party.

*"WELL, I DON'T THINK I'll ever stop being frustrated or feel fulfilled artistically."*

# Jerry Garcia

*"I MEAN, WHATEVER KILLS you kills you, and your death is authentic no matter how you die."*

(1942-1995) Jerry was the lead guitarist and primary songwriter for the Grateful Dead. His bluegrass and folk background laid the groundwork for the band, whose music eventually evolved into a wide variety of styles including blues, jazz, funk, psychedelic rock, experimental, improvisational, and even elements of disco. The band's experimental jams created a new experience for the audience at each live performance, which cultivated a loyal following of fans.

Some saw Jerry's humble and benevolent personality as a beacon in and of itself, unofficially making him the "leader" or "spokesperson" for the band, which he was never particularly comfortable with. He struggled with drugs and alcohol throughout his career and eventually succumbed to a heart attack while attending a rehabilitation facility.

# Jerry Lee Lewis

*"IF I'M GOING TO Hell, I'm going there playing*

*the piano."*

(1935-) Jerry is a rock and roll songwriter and

pianist. Nicknamed "The Killer," he was one of

the first pioneers of putting emotion into his performances and acting wild on stage. He is famous for kicking over his piano bench while playing live, and although it first happened by accident, he started deliberately incorporating it into his act. He has had 14 number one hits, and two of his songs have achieved the coveted status of being entered into the Grammy Hall of Fame. He was inducted into the Rock and Roll Hall of Fame in 1986.

# Jim Morrison

*"EXPOSE YOURSELF TO YOUR deepest fear;*

*after that, fear has no power."*

(1943-1971) Jim was the charismatic lead

singer of The Doors. His poetry and lyrical

themes were reminiscent of prominent counterculture authors like Jack Kerouac, Friedrich Nietzsche, and William Blake. His emotionally charged performances captivated audiences, and gave him status not only as a singer, but as an icon of 1960s culture.

*"I LIKE PEOPLE WHO shake other people up and make them feel uncomfortable."*

The Doors were inducted into the Rock and Roll Hall of Fame in 1993 and they have sold over 100 million records worldwide, despite their relatively short career. They were highly controversial during their heyday, but it is generally agreed upon that there was something magical about them and that they would have gone on forever had Jim not met his death at such a young age.

*"SOME OF THE WORST mistakes in my life*

*have been haircuts."*

~

*"ACTUALLY, I DON'T REMEMBER being born;*

*it must've happened during one of my blackouts."*

# Jimi Hendrix

*"YOU HAVE TO GO on and be crazy. Craziness*

*is like heaven."*

(1942-1970) Jimi was a songwriter and guitarist who has been described by many as the best rock instrumentalist who has ever lived. His style incorporated elements of rock, jazz, and blues, and he became an expert at using amp feedback to his advantage.

*"I DON'T HAVE NOTHING to regret at all in the past, except that I might've unintentionally hurt somebody else or something."*

He experimented with pedals and distortion, something that had not previously been popular. His performance as the headliner of Woodstock in 1969 is still considered to be one of the most epic and revolutionary rock performances ever.

*"I'VE BEEN IMITATED SO well, I've heard people copy my mistakes."*

During his short mainstream career, he released four albums. Since his death at the age of 27, many performances and recordings have been released posthumously. He has been the recipient of seven Grammy Hall of Fame awards, and he was inducted into the Rock and Roll Hall of Fame in 1992.

*"IT'S FUNNY HOW MOST people love the dead; once you're dead, you're made for life."*

# Jimmy Page

*"I MAY NOT BELIEVE in myself, but I believe in*

*what I'm doing."*

(1944-) Jimmy is a guitarist, songwriter, and record producer best known for being the founder and guitarist for Led Zeppelin. He began his career as a prolific and highly-sought session musician, and was eventually recruited to be part of The Yardbirds. It was during his time with The Yardbirds that he became connected with prominent artists like Jeff Beck and also Keith Moon and John Entwistle of The Who. He met bassist John Paul Jones during this time, who eventually connected him with Robert Plant and John Bonham, thus rounding out the lineup who would become Led Zeppelin. Led Zeppelin went on to become the second best-selling band in the US.

# Joan Baez

*"I'VE NEVER HAD A humble opinion. If you've*

*got an opinion, why be humble about it?"*

(1941-) Joan first became famous in the 1960s

as a folk singer and songwriter. Her career has

spanned five decades, and she has released over 30 albums. In more recent times, she has enjoyed creating her own interpretations of songs by other artists. She also is a prominent activist and has been seen at many protests and political events. Amnesty International named an award after her in 2011, which is given each year to an artist who fights for human rights. She has become relatively quiet lately, preferring to spend time alone in nature and with her family.

# Joan Jett

*"GIRLS HAVE GOT BALLS. They're just a little*

*higher up that's all."*

(1958-) A teenaged Joan first rose to prominence when she formed The Runaways in 1975. They toured with other bands as an opening act and produced five albums but never saw a high level of success in the US. Most of their popularity was abroad, especially in Japan.

*"NOBODY KNOWS WHAT ANTICIPATION is anymore. Everything is so immediate."*

Following the breakup of the Runaways, Joan struck out on her own and eventually created her band, The Blackhearts. In addition to creating multiple hits with The Blackhearts, she has also collaborated with and produced for other artists. She is an avid activist for animal rights. She has not yet been inducted into the Rock and Roll Hall of Fame, although she has been nominated twice.

# Joe Cocker

*"GOD, I'M JUST A fat bald guy, 60 years old,*

*singing the blues, you know?"*

(1944-) Joe is a blues and rock singer, most

famous for his covers of other artists' work. He

brings a new spin to every track he covers and has created many popular renditions of songs by The Beatles. His gritty voice is unmistakable, and his live performances are a sight to behold, as he writhes and dances in an almost spastic way. He has released 22 albums, and he won a Grammy in 1983 for his duet with Jennifer Warnes, "Up Where We Belong."

# Joe Perry

*"A BAND ISN'T A band unless they're playing together. Otherwise, it's just five guys that are living off their royalty checks."*

(1950-) Joe is the lead guitarist of Aerosmith. He and Aerosmith's lead singer, Steven Tyler, have been longtime friends, but have also had a contentious relationship that has been reflected in the band's work and success.

Their blues-rock style resonated well with audiences in the 1970s, and their first five albums were commercial hits. The early 1980s were a struggle for Joe and Steven, who both partied hard and earned the nickname "The Toxic Twins." Aerosmith briefly broke up before reuniting in the late 1980s and getting back to their mega-hit, rock superstar status. Joe has also been a successful solo artist and a collaborator on many albums for others.

# Joe Strummer

*"THE TOUGHEST THING IS facing yourself.*

*Being honest with yourself, that's much tougher*

*than beating someone up. That's what I call*

*tough."*

(1952-2002) Born John Graham Mellor, Joe was the lyricist and lead singer of The Clash. The Clash was part of the punk movement that overtook the UK in the late 1970s into the 1980s. They combined punk with many other styles, including reggae, ska, funk, rockabilly, and an early form of rap, which made their music different from the rest of the British punk bands. Throughout his career, Joe played with several other bands and recorded as a solo artist as well He was inducted into the Rock and Roll Hall of Fame, along with The Clash, in 2001.

# Joey Ramone

*"I ENJOYED MY LIFE when I had nothing... and kinda like the idea of just being happy with me."*

(1951-2001) Born Jeffrey Ross Hyman, Joey was the lead singer of punk band The Ramones. He had no formal vocal training, which gave way to his signature style, cracks, hiccups, bleats, and all. No other rock band at the time had such a distinctive vocalist. His image became iconic with the punk movement. The Ramones toured almost constantly for 22 years, finally disbanding in 1996 after a performance at the Lollapalooza festival. They were inducted into the Rock and Roll Hall of Fame in 2002.

# John Bonham

*"MY NERVES BEFORE A gig got worse; I had*

*terrible bad nerves all the time. Once we*

*started... I was fine."*

(1948-1980) John was the drummer for Led

Zeppelin and is considered by many to be one of

the best rock drummers of all time. He is known for his natural talent and instinct, and for creating techniques and rhythms that could never be taught, only felt. He was technically brilliant and had mastered many different styles at his young age, including Latin, reggae, and funk. His death at the age of 32 came as a great shock to many, and the group decided to disband rather than try to replace him.

*"SOMETIMES, TOURING GETS A bit wearing, but that's only because I'm married with kids at home. I've never gotten pissed off with the actual touring. I enjoy playing – I could play every night. It's just being away that gets you down sometimes. I still enjoy going through different towns that we haven't been to before. But you get*

*fed up with places like New York because they're*

*not interesting anymore."*

# John Cale

*"IF I'M INTERESTED IN what I'm doing, other people will be interested in it."*

(1942-) John Cale OBE is best known as a founding member and multi-instrumentalist for experimental rock band The Velvet Underground. John's background was mostly in classical music and composing, but when he met Lou Reed in 1964, he found that the two of them shared an interest in rock music. Together, they embarked on an experiment that not only included guitar, bass, and drums, but also instruments that were non-traditional for a rock band like the viola. Their new approach to music influenced many bands that came after them. They were inducted into the Rock and Roll Hall of Fame in 1996.

# John Coltrane

*"YOU CAN PLAY A shoestring if you're*

*sincere."*

(1926-1967) John was both a jazz saxophonist

and composer. In addition to recording his own

work and creating the new concept at the time of

"free form jazz," he also frequently collaborated with other jazz legends, including Miles Davis and Thelonious Monk. His legacy paved the way for other jazz musicians as well as for bands like the Grateful Dead who would eventually become known for their experimentation and improvisation. John was posthumously awarded a Grammy for one of his live performances, in addition to winning the Grammy Lifetime Achievement Award.

# John Fogerty

*"THE FACT THAT THERE are a lot of good songs means there are also a lot of really bad songs I've written that you never hear."*

(1945-) John is best known as the guitarist and lead singer for Creedence Clearwater Revival (CCR). Their raw style of blues-rock resonated with many during the late 1960s, and enabled them to have a great deal of commercial success. They have sold over 26 million albums worldwide and were inducted into the Rock and Roll Hall of Fame in 1993. Tension among band members and John's belief that he should have more creative control caused them to disband in 1972, but John has since had a successful solo career.

*"I USUALLY DESTROY UNRELEASED material. It has a way of coming back to haunt you."*

# John Lennon

*"LIFE IS WHAT HAPPENS while you are busy*

*making other plans."*

(1940-1980) As a founding member of the

Beatles, John rose to meteoric fame in the 1960s.

His songwriting partnership with fellow founding

member Paul McCartney is still considered to be one of the most powerful and creative partnerships in history.

*"REALITY LEAVES A LOT to the imagination."*

While his earlier songs were simpler and more about creating a pop sound that would attract fans, his later work reflected more of his emotions and true beliefs. He was an adamant pacifist and political activist. He also experimented heavily with LSD, which began to reflect in his work, especially after the breakup of the Beatles.

*"TIME YOU ENJOY WASTING was not wasted."*

Although his career had begun to take a very different turn, his murder at the age of 40 was a tragic loss for the music industry and for the creative world in general. Even listeners and critics who were not fans of his later work could not deny his courage and vulnerability as an artist. He had a tremendous influence on many musicians who came after him.

*"I'M NOT CLAIMING DIVINITY. I've never claimed purity of soul. I've never claimed to have the answers to life. I only put out songs to answer questions as honestly as I can... But I still believe in peace, love, and understanding."*

~

*"MUSIC IS EVERYBODY'S POSSESSION. It's*

*only publishers who think that people own it."*

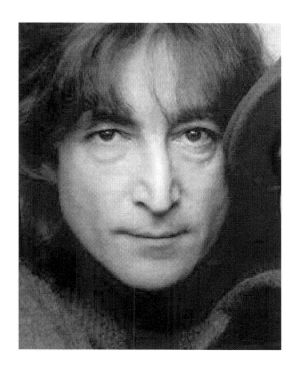

# John Lydon

*"GOSSIP IS A VERY dangerous tool. We should*

*be more wary of the gossiper, and not the gossip*

*they're trying to relay to you."*

(1956) Better known by his stage name, Johnny Rotten, John is the former lead singer of the Sex Pistols and current lead singer of Public Image Ltd. John made an image for himself by generally causing an uproar. His lyrics were frequently critical of the British Royal Family, and he and his band would openly curse on stage and in televised performances. He and the Sex Pistols took punk music to a new level by adhering to a true punk attitude. Right in line with this attitude, he and the rest of the band refused to attend the ceremony when they were inducted into the Rock and Roll Hall of Fame in 2006, even going so far as to call the institution a "piss stain."

# John Mayer

*"HIGH SCHOOL IS LIKE a spork: it's a crappy spoon and a crappy fork, so in the end it's just plain useless."*

(1977-) John is a singer-songwriter known for his acoustic rock style that incorporates a bit of a blues twist. He was launched into fame by the South by Southwest Festival, held each year in Austin, Texas. His 2000 performance at the festival attracted the attention of several record companies, and he was an instant commercial success. He loves to collaborate with other artists, including artists outside his typical genre. He is also an avid activist, particularly for environmental causes. He has won seven Grammy awards out of 19 nominations.

*"WHO I AM AS a guitarist is defined by my failure to become Jimi Hendrix."*

# John Rzeznik

*"IF LIFE HANDS YOU a lemon, throw it at*

*someone."*

(1965-) John is best known as the lead singer and guitarist for the Goo Goo Dolls. While they saw the height of their popularity in the late 1990s and early 2000s, they are still recording new music and touring. They have had 14 top ten singles across several different charts, and they have sold over 10 million albums worldwide. Their songs have appeared on numerous television and movie soundtracks, and they have been nominated for four Grammy awards.

# Johnny Cash

*"SUCCESS IS HAVING TO worry about every*

*damn thing in the world, except money."*

(1932-2003) Born simply J.R. Cash, Johnny

became a blues and folk songwriting legend. His

deep baritone vocals are distinctive, even when heard in unexpected ways, such as on his last album when he covered multiple songs written by artists of the 20th century.

*"THE THINGS THAT HAVE always been important: to be a good man, to try to live my life the way God would have me, to turn it over to Him that His will might be worked in my life, to do my work without looking back, to give it all I've got, and to take pride in my work as an honest performer."*

Johnny was known for his humble attitude and for using music as a means of communication and storytelling. Some of his most iconic performances were free concerts that were held at prisons. He advocated for prison reform and for standing up for those who couldn't stand up for themselves, and he spoke freely about his struggle with drug addiction.

*"YOU BUILD ON FAILURE. You use it as a stepping stone. Close the door on the past. You don't try to forget the mistakes, but you don't dwell on it. You don't let it have any of your energy, or any of your time, or any of your space."*

He has won 19 Grammy awards including three Grammy Hall of Fame awards. Some of his notable awards are not for his music at all, but rather for videos, spoken word, and his self-penned liner notes. He was inducted into the Rock and Roll Hall of Fame in 1992.

# Jon Anderson

*"I THINK IF YOU let go of preconceived ideas,*

*you'll find everything in this life."*

(1944-) Jon is best known as the former lead singer for Yes, although he has also had a prolific career as solo artist and collaborator. Yes was most popular in the 1970s, as their sound had a progressive edge that had not been explored by many other artists at the time. Yes's innovation and experimentation introduced audiences to new ideas, thus paving the way for bands like Genesis, Rush, and Pink Floyd.

Jon's singing style falls into the high end of the tenor range, leading many to believe that he sings in falsetto. The combination of his unusual voice, mystical lyrics, and complicated compositions made Yes an interesting band to follow. They have gone through multiple lineup changes throughout their history and are touring today with only one remaining original member.

# Jon Bon Jovi

*"MIRACLES HAPPEN EVERY DAY. Change your perception of what a miracle is, and you'll see them all around you."*

(1962-) Jon is a singer and songwriter, primarily known as the front man of Bon Jovi. Bon Jovi's success began at the grassroots level, with a local New York radio station recognizing their talent. It took a year to finalize their lineup, but their rise to fame was quick, especially after the release of *Slippery When Wet*. While they started as a straight-up rock band, their image and style have changed over the years, incorporating more serious lyrics and elements of country music into their songs. They have released 12 studio albums, which have gone on to sell over 100 million copies worldwide.

# Jonathan Davis

*"YOU LAUGH AT ME because I'm different, I laugh at you because you're all the same."*

(1971-) Sometimes known by his DJ stage moniker, JDevil, Jonathan is the lead singer for Korn. Considered to be the pioneers of "nu metal," Korn first hit mainstream success in the late 1990s. They have gone on to win two

Grammys and sell over 35 million records worldwide. Their no-holds-barred approach to music has influenced many other legendary bands, including Rage Against the Machine, Nine Inch Nails, Jane's Addiction, Primus, and the Red Hot Chili Peppers. Combining heavy riffs with elements of hip-hop, rap, and funk became their signature style, and when paired with their unapologetic lyrics, their music makes a tremendous impact.

# Joni Mitchell

*"FAME IS A SERIES of misunderstandings*

*surrounding a name."*

(1943-) Joni is a singer-songwriter who broke

out in the folk genre, but has since expanded into

blues, rock, jazz, and some experimentation with

non-Western sounds. She is often known for her vocals and her lyrical vulnerability, but she is also an accomplished and technical guitarist.

*"SORROW IS SO EASY to express and yet so hard to tell."*

Many artists have been influenced by her work, and many have gone on to produce critically acclaimed cover versions of her songs. She is also known for her political and environmental activism. She has won eight Grammy awards in 15 nominations.

# Justin Timberlake

*"I GET WAY MORE nervous playing golf in front*

*of 500 people than being on stage in front of*

*20,000 people."*

(1981-) Justin has had a long history in the entertainment industry, beginning with his appearances on *Star Search* and *The Mickey Mouse Club* as a child. He then went on to be part of the international superstar boy band, NSYNC. Since the group parted ways in 2002, Justin has released four studio albums as a solo artist, and he has become almost as well-known for his acting roles as he has for his music. He is one of few artists to have both Emmy and Grammy awards to his name. Across all award platforms, he has been nominated 117 times, of which he has won 60, making him one of the most successful entertainers ever.

# Kathleen Hanna

*"ART REVOLVES AROUND CREATING*

*something that isn't there."*

(1968-) Kathleen is the former lead singer of punk bands Bikini Kill and Le Tigre. She is known for being an outspoken feminist. She is considered to be one of the founders of the riot grrrl movement, which emphasized lo-fi, do-it-yourself production values and attitudes, and also female empowerment.

Kathleen and Bikini Kill, along with other bands in the riot grrrl movement wanted to ensure that their shows and events would be safe places for women and places that would give women a platform to speak freely about their issues. She is also an avid writer and has been a frequent contributor to various punk and feminist magazines.

# Keith Moon

*"I TOLD PEOPLE I was a drummer before I*

*even had a set, I was a mental drummer."*

(1946-1978) Keith was the wildly talented but

often ill-behaved and uncontrollable drummer for

The Who. His style was unique and energetic, like

John Bonham's, but it is often said that he got by

302

on sheer talent rather than having much discipline for the craft. He also was known for his destructive lifestyle both onstage and off. He was particularly notorious for trashing hotel rooms and putting explosives in toilets. Despite his talent, he was never able to remain focused for very long, and he slipped into long benders of drugs and alcohol. Finally, in an attempt to get sober, he died form an overdose of Heminevrin, which was a drug used to curb the effects of alcohol detoxification.

# Keith Richards

*"I'VE NEVER HAD A problem with drugs. I've*

*had problems with the police."*

(1943-) Keith is the guitarist for the Rolling

Stones. He and lead singer Mick Jagger write

together and have become one of the most

influential songwriting duos in rock music. Keith

also has done several albums as a solo artist and frequently collaborates with other musicians.

*"IT'S GREAT TO BE here. It's great to be anywhere."*

He had some legal troubles throughout the Rolling Stones's early career mainly due to his substance use, but he has since calmed down, despite his public image of being a wild man. In fact, he is an avid reader and is working towards turning his massive book collection into a library.

*"I LOOK FOR AMBIGUITY when I'm writing because life is ambiguous."*

~

*"I MEAN SOME DOCTOR told me I had six*

*months to live and I went to their funeral."*

~

*"IF YOU'RE GOING TO kick authority in the*

*teeth, you might as well use both feet."*

~

*"TO ME, MY BIGGEST fear is getting a big*

*head, and that is when I get the hammer. Because*

*it's very easy in this game to believe you're*

*something special.* "

# Krist Novoselić

*"WHENEVER HISTORY IS IN the making,*

*there's some kind of intangible feeling."*

(1965-) Krist is best known as one of the founding members and the bassist of Nirvana. He and singer Kurt Cobain met through Krist's older brother, and when the two realized their similar tastes in music, the teamed up and started a band. Nirvana had a short career due to Kurt Cobain's death, but they are widely regarded as one of the most influential bands in history. They were one of the pioneers of grunge rock and went on to have enormous mainstream success. Following the disbanding of Nirvana, Krist played with a couple of other bands, but has focused more of his energy on political activism and writing.

# Kurt Cobain

*"WANTING TO BE SOMEONE else is a waste of the person you are."*

(1967-1994) Kurt was the founder and lead singer of Nirvana. Nirvana became hailed as "the flagship band" of Generation X, and with Kurt as its assumed leader, he was considered to be "the spokesman of a generation." He was never very comfortable with all of his praise and media attention, and he was frequently concerned that Nirvana's music was being misconstrued and misinterpreted by fans and the press.

*"I REALLY HAVEN'T HAD that exciting of a life. There are a lot of things I wish I would have done, instead of just sitting around and complaining about having a boring life. So I pretty much like to make it up. I'd rather tell a story about somebody else."*

Kurt's volatile relationship with wife Courtney Love was a frequent topic for media coverage, another aspect of fame that Kurt disliked. Nirvana disbanded in 1994 after Kurt's death, which was ruled a suicide. In their seven-year career, they released three studio albums, which have sold over 75 million copies worldwide. They were inducted into the Rock and Roll Hall of Fame in 2014.

# Lars Ulrich

*"EVERY TIME WE PUT a record out, we lose people that can't deal with the growth."*

(1963-) Lars is best known as the drummer for Metallica. Early in his career with Metallica, he was praised for his speed and apparent technical skill, but his later simplification of his drumbeats have caused critics to call his skill into question. To fans, he is known for his quick and precise use of the double bass pedal and for his heavy playing style.

Many rock drummers have cited Lars as an influence and inspiration. Lars has also been an outspoken opponent of music piracy, contributing to the decline of the peer-to-peer sharing site, Napster. Metallica's commercial success is unmatched by any other heavy metal band; they have sold over 120 million records worldwide. They are said to be working on their tenth studio album, which has a tentative 2015 release date.

# Leonard Cohen

*"ACT THE WAY YOU'D like to be and soon*

*you'll be the way you act."*

(1934-) Leonard is a singer-songwriter who has also gained accolades for his poetry and novels. His 1984 song, "Hallelujah," has been covered by over 200 artists in multiple different languages. Possibly the most famous version was rendered by the late Jeff Buckley, which became one of his most popular and sought-after recordings. His songs and writings cover a diverse range of topics, such as love, politics, depression, and other sensitive subjects many artists shy away from. He has toured extensively, released 13 studio albums, written two novels, and published fifteen collections of poetry. He was inducted into the Rock and Roll Hall of Fame in 2008.

# Levon Helm

*"SONGS DON'T WEAR OUT. Good songs are good now. If they were a comfort during those hard times in the past, they'll be a comfort in today's age."*

(1940-2012) Levon is best known as the lead singer and multi-instrumentalist for The Band. The Band's career began as Bob Dylan's touring and backing band. They eventually decided that they wanted to try writing and performing their own material, and thus forged a career by themselves.

*"I DON'T FOOL WITH a lot of things that I can't have fun with. There's not much reward in that."*

Their style was based in blues-rock, although Levon's slight southern accent brought a hint of country to the music. Many legendary bands cite The Band as an influence, including the Grateful Dead, Led Zeppelin, Crosby, Stills & Nash, the Black Crowes, the Wallflowers, and even more modern bands like The Shins, Ween, and Wilco.

They were inducted into the Rock and Roll Hall of Fame in 1994.

*"IF YOU POUR SOME music on whatever's wrong, it'll sure help out."*

# Little Richard

*"I ALSO THINK THAT what's wrong with all of us is that we don't show enough love toward each other."*

(1932-) Born Richard Wayne Penniman, Little Richard has had a prolific career that has spanned six decades. His career began in the gospel world, but turned to rock and roll and rhythm & blues after the initial success of his first performance of "Tutti Frutti."

*"GAY PEOPLE ARE THE sweetest, kindest, most artistic, warmest and most thoughtful people in the world. And since the beginning of time all they've ever been is kicked."*

His flamboyant performance style became famous onto itself and laid the groundwork for influencing various early rock musicians. His religious convictions are frequently brought into discussions about him, and he has made the switch back and forth between gospel and secular music several times. He is a legend and is considered to be one of the founding fathers of modern rock and roll. He was inducted into the Rock and Roll Hall of Fame in 1986 and won the Grammy Lifetime Achievement Award in 1993.

*"IF I HAD MY life to live over, I would want to be a man."*

# Lou Reed

*"I'M VERY EMOTIONALLY AFFECTED by*

*sound. Sounds are the inexplicable… There is a*

*sound you hear in your head, it's your nerves or*

*your blood running."*

(1942-2013) Lou began his career as the lead singer and primary songwriter for The Velvet Underground, but is perhaps best known for his solo work following the breakup of the band. The Velvet Underground was "ahead of their time" in that they were not commercially successful while they were together, but many prominent bands have cited them as an influence.

Lou's unusual vocal style certainly contributed to his influence and legacy. There was something almost unmusical about it, but it was genuine and communicative nonetheless. Lou was inducted into the Rock and Roll Hall of Fame with The Velvet Underground, and although he has been nominated twice as a solo artist, he has not yet been inducted.

# Madonna

*"POWER IS BEING TOLD you are not loved and*

*not being destroyed by it. "*

(1958-) Known as the "Queen of Pop,"

Madonna revolutionized the music industry,

especially for women. She is the best-selling female artist of all time, having sold over 300 million records worldwide. Her provocative style in both her fashion sense and her music caused an uproar and made her a controversial artist of her time, but also contributed to her popularity and influence.

She has written and produced most of her own songs, which is unusual for a pop star. She has become a successful actress and fashion designer in addition to continuing to create albums and tour. She has won seven Grammy awards out of 28 nominations, and she was inducted into the Rock and Roll Hall of Fame in 2008.

# Marilyn Manson

*"YOU GET DEPRESSED BECAUSE you know*

*that you are not what you should be."*

(1969-) Born Brian Hugh Warner, Marilyn is

best known as the lead singer of heavy metal band

Marilyn Manson. They have been no strangers to controversy and have been accused of being a negative influence on young people, particularly in the context of the 1999 shooting at Columbine High School.

*"A LOT OF PEOPLE don't want to make their own decisions. They're too scared. It's much easier to be told what to do."*

Marilyn has often been asked to respond to these claims, during which he explains that he recognizes that his music and public image are provocative, but that he is in no way encouraging violence. He has been nominated for four

Grammy awards and is also an avid and talented visual artist.

*"IN ANY STORY, THE villain is the catalyst. The hero's not a person who will bend the rules or show the cracks in his armor. He's one-dimensional intentionally, but the villain is the person who owns up to what he is and stands by it."*

~

*"I NEVER SAID TO be like me. I said to be like you and make a difference."*

~

*"THERE'S NO REASON TO change what you are, but if you're not being you, then you need to acknowledge that."*

# Mark Hoppus

*"MAKE YOURSELF LOOK REALLY stupid so you don't feel bad doing something a little stupid."*

(1972-) Mark is best known as the bassist and co-lead vocalist for Blink-182. He and guitarist Tom DeLonge started the band together in 1993, but they first achieved mainstream commercial success with their 1999 album *Enema of the State*. Mark and Tom have had creative differences over the years, leading to a long hiatus of the band, but they reunited in 2009 and have released two albums since. Mark also has appeared on television as an actor and music commentator, and he owns his own clothing line.

# Matt Bellamy

*"PART OF ME JUST wants to blow up the world!*

*It's all crap! And part of me thinks, 'Mmm I want*

*to be in love with everyone!'"*

(1978-) Matt is the lead singer and multi-instrumentalist for progressive rock band Muse. Matt's talent for composing comes out in Muse's music, which covers genres such as space-rock, electronica, alternative, and symphonic rock. They are particularly known for their energetic and visually intense live performances. They have sold over 15 million albums worldwide and they have won one Grammy award.

# Michael Franti

*"YOU LEARN A LOT when you're barefoot. The first thing is every step you take is different."*

(1966-) Michael is a poet and singer, best known as the lead singer for his band, Michael

Franti & Spearhead. His long dreadlocks and penchant for traveling barefoot make him easily recognizable. His music combines hip-hop with other styles, including reggae, folk, rock, and funk, and his lyrics are often politically charged. He is an avid activist for both environmental and political causes, even going so far as to not allow disposable water bottles at his shows or on tours. He has released eight studio albums and has been part of numerous collaborations.

# Michael Hutchence

*"IT'S JUST AS DIFFICULT to live in a self-made hell of privacy as it is to live in a self-made hell of publicity."*

(1960-1997) Michael was best known as the lead singer and lyricist for INXS. Their new wave sound brought something different that both surprised and captivated audiences. Michael was always considered to be a charismatic and magnetic performer, and his personality helped create a loyal fan following. Michael's suicide in 1997 was a huge blow to the band and to the music industry in general, who felt like they had lost a true creative genius.

*"WOMEN ARE INCREDIBLE IN groups together. Terrifying. Men have nothing on them."*

The band eventually continued with a variety of other lead singers, but most fans and critics agree that things were never the same without Michael. INXS has sold over 40 million records worldwide.

# Michael Jackson

*"IF YOU ENTER THIS world knowing you are*

*loved and you leave this world knowing the same,*

*then everything that happens in between can be*

*dealt with."*

(1958-2009) Widely known as the "King of Pop," Michael was a singer and dancer who started his career with his brothers in The Jackson 5. He eventually went on to have one of the most successful solo careers of any artist ever. He has broken numerous world records for album sales, and his 1982 album *Thriller* remains the best selling album of all time.

He, along with Madonna, changed the music industry by using music videos as a means for connecting with fans and presenting music in a visual way. His electric dance moves and magnetic stage presence enabled him to create videos that not only changed the way people experienced music, but that also broke through racial barriers like no other artist before him had been able to.

Odd stories from his personal life sometimes overshadowed his music career, but no one could deny that he was a creative force to be reckoned with. He died of cardiac arrest while in rehearsals for what was to be his last tour before retiring. He has 19 Grammy awards and was inducted into the Rock and Roll Hall of Fame twice – with The Jackson 5 in 1997, and as a solo artist in 2001.

# Michael Schenker

*"I PRACTICED FOR AT least two hours every day for twenty years, before then I practiced maybe four to five hours a day, and before then 14 hours a day. It was all I had ever done."*

(1955-) Michael and his older brother, Rudolf, were early members of the Scorpions (really early – Michael was only 11 years old at their first gig!). After the Scorpions's tour that supported their first album, Michael was recruited to be the lead guitarist for UFO. After a turbulent stint with UFO and a brief reunion with the Scorpions, Michael embarked on his solo career.

He has struggled with alcohol abuse and reckless behavior throughout his career, but his playing has always been well-respected by other musicians. Many cite him as an influence, and he has been invited to audition for Aerosmith, the Rolling Stones, and Ozzy Osbourne.

# Michael Stipe

*"NEVER EAT BROCCOLI WHEN there are*

*cameras around."*

(1960-) Michael Stipe is best known as the former lead singer for R.E.M. He also was the band's primary lyricist and graphic artist throughout their career. His often quick and mumbling singing style was distinctive and always tended to be a source of great praise or great criticism for the band.

He enjoyed exploring lyrical concepts that were personally meaningful to him at the time, including politics, the environment, religion, mass culture, love, and mysticism. He has collaborated with many musicians and film directors, and he has also produced several albums and films. R.E.M. was inducted into the Rock and Roll Hall of Fame in 2007.

# Mick Jagger

*"LOSE YOUR DREAMS, AND you might lose*

*your mind."*

(1943-) Mick is the co-founder and lead

singer for the Rolling Stones. His unusual

performance style seemed to cross the boundaries

of stereotypical masculine movement, which gave him an early reputation as a counterculture figure.

*"I AM NOT A librarian of my own work. It's a good thing not to be too involved with what you have done."*

His stage persona went on to influence huge icons like Iggy Pop, Jim Morrison, and David Bowie. Currently, the Rolling Stones are still touring, much to the surprise of veteran musicians, who constantly praise Mick and Keith for their strength, stamina, and seemingly endless youth. The Rolling Stones were inducted into the Rock and Roll Hall of Fame in 1989 and have sold over 250 million records worldwide.

# Mike Dirnt

*"I'M AN OPTIMISTIC AGNOSTIC. I think the*

*second we die, within a matter of seconds,*

*everybody else arrives, and that's the party, and*

*you live your hell on earth."*

(1972-) Mike is the bassist and occasional vocalist for Green Day. Gaining mainstream popularity in the early 1990s, Green Day is often considered to be one of the bands that made punk commercially accessible. Some praise them for this, while others think it goes against the very nature of "punk."

They branched out beyond punk with their album *American Idiot*, which was a rock opera, similar to The Who's *Tommy*. It was adapted for stage production and went on to win two Tony awards. Green Day has sold over 75 million albums worldwide, and they have won five Grammys.

# Mike Gordon

*"TAKE ALL OF YOUR ideas and follow through*

*with them all of the way."*

(1965-) Mike is best known as the bassist and one of the founding members of Phish. He has written many of their songs and was also their public relations manager for many years. He has frequently collaborated with other musicians, releasing several albums as a solo artist or as part of a duo or group. His extensive musical knowledge has helped Phish pull influence from various genres, including rock, folk, funk, Latin, bluegrass, jazz, psychedelic, and even traditional Jewish music. While they are primarily known for their elaborate live tours, they have also released 12 studio albums.

# Mike Herrera

*"EVERYBODY'S CRAZY IN SOME way and*

*everybody's weird, and that kind of makes us all*

*the same in a lot of ways. We're not alone, we just*

*think we are."*

(1976-) Mike is the bassist and lead singer for punk band MxPx. Their earlier albums reflected Christian lyrics and themes, putting them in the category of Christian punk or Christian rock, but they have since shed this influence. Mike enjoys playing different types of music and also currently fronts a band called Tumbledown, which has more of a country vibe. With MxPx, Mike recorded nine studio albums, one of which has been certified Gold by the RIAA.

# Mike Shinoda

*"I GOT OVER BEING embarrassed."*

(1977-) Mike is best known as the rapper and primary songwriter for Linkin Park. He is also a multi-instrumentalist, providing keyboards and rhythm guitar for the band. He has been involved in almost every aspect of production for Linkin Park, including album artwork, production, and engineering. His passion for the technical side of recording has made him a respected and sought-out producer and consultant. He also fronts a band called Fort Minor, in which he displays more of his hip-hop roots.

# Miley Cyrus

*"IT'S SO MUCH EASIER to know who you are*

*when there aren't a thousand people telling you*

*who they think you are."*

(1992-) Born Destiny Hope Cyrus, she legally

changed her name to reflect her childhood

nickname, "Miley," a reference to the fact that she was often smiling. She began her career as the star of the hit teen show *Hannah Montana* and performed on several tours as her title character from the show.

As she began to focus more on music instead of acting, she began to shift her image away from the wholesome Hannah Montana character and began to take on a unique style of her own. Her album, *Bangerz*, released in 2013, was accompanied by multiple controversial performances that have brought up comparisons to Madonna and her provocative nature. Miley currently holds four Guinness World Records.

# Moby

*"DOGS HAVE BOUNDLESS ENTHUSIASM but no sense of shame. I should have a dog as a life coach."*

(1965-) Born Richard Melville Hall, Moby is a singer-songwriter and DJ. His work with electronic dance music (EDM) in the early 1990s brought that genre to the mainstream and influenced many EDM artists after him. He also frequently collaborates with other artists, particularly with the purpose of re-mixing current songs. He is very public about his support for animal rights and is a strict vegan. He has been nominated for six Grammy awards.

# Morrissey

*"MADONNA REINFORCES EVERYTHING*

*ABSURD and offensive. Desperate womanhood.*

*Madonna is closer to organized prostitution than*

*anything else."*

(1959-) Known primarily by only his last name, Steven Patrick Morrissey is a singer-songwriter who was the lead singer of The Smiths, and currently is a solo artist. The Smiths became popular in the 1980s as an alternative rock band. Their focus on basic rock instruments was a sharp contrast to the synth-heavy Britpop that was dominating the airwaves at the time. His solo work continues and expands upon that style. He is often cited as an influence by other musicians, both for his musical work and for his outspoken ideals and opinions. He is a vehement animal rights activist.

# Nancy Wilson

*"EVEN THOUGH THERE ARE really no original themes or stories to tell, it's more about the way you tell the story."*

(1954-) Nancy, along with her older sister Ann, is one of the core members of Heart. Nancy provides backing vocals and powerful harmonies with her sister, in addition to playing the guitar. Heart has had incredible commercial success throughout their career, selling over 35 million albums worldwide. The dynamic between Ann and Nancy is often cited as a reason for their success, as well as their ability to bring multiple styles of music together in one song, increasing their fan appeal. They were inducted into the Rock and Roll Hall of Fame in 2013.

# Nate Ruess

*"AS LONG AS YOU'RE creating the art you want*

*to create, if people start liking you, you shouldn't*

*have to apologize. You want your stuff to be*

*heard by as many people as possible."*

(1982-) Nate has been a staple in the indie

music scene for over a decade, but is best known

as the current lead singer of Fun. His distinctive

singing style and heartfelt lyrics have helped Fun. become an enormous commercial success.

*"WELL THE CRAZY THING for me is I think out of anything that's happened in the last year, all the success, people always ask, 'what do you guys do with the money?' I don't think they realize we're not really making any money."*

Their 2012 album *Some Nights* has received a lot of attention, with several of the songs being used in films and television shows. It has been certified Platinum in five countries. Fun. has won two Grammy awards in six nominations.

*"LYRICS HAVE BECOME SO dumbed down nowadays. People don't want to have to think about lyrics anymore, they just want to be told something. Until these great things started happening with us, I'd really given up on reaching people like that."*

*"I ALWAYS WANTED TO be a singer, but none of my friends thought I could sing."*

# Neil Peart

*"THERE'S STILL A LOT I'm angry about: a lot*

*of human behaviour that's appalling and*

*despicable, but you choose what you fight*

*against. I always thought if I could just put*

*something into words perfectly enough, people*

*would get the idea and it would change things."*

(1952-) Neil is a musician and author, best known as the drummer and lyricist for Rush. He is often praised for his incredible technical skill, particularly his ability to seamlessly weave together different time signatures.

*"TOO MUCH ATTENTION AND hoopla doesn't agree with my temperament."*

He is also famous for his precision and stamina. In addition to his drumming ability, he is the author of all of Rush's lyrics, which have been known to cover a wide variety of subjects, including social consciousness, war, the environment, human emotion, literature, and science fiction. He frequently appears near the top of lists of "greatest rock drummers of all time."

*"PLAYING A THREE-HOUR Rush show is like running a marathon while solving equations."*

*"TO GET NOSTALGIC ABOUT other people's music, or even about your own, makes a terrible statement about the condition of your life and your prospects for the future."*

# Neil Young

*"WHEN PEOPLE START ASKING you to do the same thing over and over again, that's when you know you're way too close to something that you don't want to be near."*

(1945-) Neil is a singer-songwriter who has been successful as a solo artist and who also performed as a member of Buffalo Springfield and Crosby, Stills, Nash & Young. He is a technically proficient guitar player and writes deeply personal lyrics.

His style is eclectic: sometimes leaning towards blues, jazz, and folk, while tending more towards heavy alternative rock at others. He has contributed to films both as a musician and as a director. He is an avid environmentalist and is one of the founders of the Farm Aid festival. He has won two Grammy awards, and he has been inducted into the Rock and Roll Hall of Fame twice: in 1995 as a solo artist, and in 1997 as a member of Buffalo Springfield.

# Nikki Sixx

*"I USED TO THINK the only way to be truly*

*alive is to confront your mortality."*

(1958-) Born Frank Carlton Serafino Feranna Jr., Nikki is the bassist and lead songwriter for Mötley Crüe. He also has been part of multiple collaborations and solo projects. Mötley Crüe is considered to be one of the pioneers of glam metal, along with bands such as Van Halen, Bon Jovi, Quiet Riot, and Ratt.

*"I WAS SO HAPPY every morning when I woke up that I was pissing smiley faces."*

Nikki thrived in the glam metal scene and basked in the excessive lifestyle that went along with the music. He struggled with heroin addiction, overdosing multiple times. This experience became the inspiration for his autobiography: *The Heroin Diaries: A Year in the Life of a Shattered Rock Star.* He continues to make music with various groups, including Mötley Crüe, and he also owns a clothing line and hosts a radio show.

*"I MEAN, YOU CAN hate us. I don't care if you hate us, but no one will ever sound like us."*

# Noel Gallagher

*"I ABSOLUTELY LOVED BEING famous. It was*

*all great, up until the point when it wasn't."*

(1967-) Noel is singer-songwriter, best known as the former guitarist and songwriter for Oasis. Oasis, along with Blur, was one of the principal bands in the Britpop movement of the 1990s.

*"AMERICANS ARE CRAZY. THEY have this fascination with throwing their shoes on stage. I've been to a lot of shows in me life, some good and some bad. But I was never moved to take off me shoes and throw it at the lead singer."*

Their catchy riffs and power chords were reminiscent of the Beatles, and they went on to sell over 70 million albums worldwide. Despite their popularity and meteoric rise to commercial success, Noel and his brother Liam, who was the lead singer of the band, frequently had violent disputes, ultimately leading to the breakup of the band. Noel started his own musical project and has continued to influence artists with his songwriting and singing styles.

# Otis Redding

*"IF I WERE TO leave the U.S., I'd live in England. But I'd never leave the U.S. I own a 400-acre farm in Macon, Georgia. I raise cattle and hogs. I own horses, too. I love horses as much as singing. I like to hunt on horseback."*

(1941-1967) Otis began his career as part of Little Richard's backing band, but eventually became noticed as a talented and soulful singer. He was one of the first African-American artists to gain appeal on a national level. His songs, "(Sittin' On) The Dock of the Bay," "Try a Little Tenderness," and "Respect" are known worldwide and have influenced many artists. His sudden death in a plane crash at the age of 26 was a huge loss to the music industry, especially to Stax Records and the soul genre. He was posthumously awarded the Grammy Lifetime Achievement Award, and he was inducted into the Rock and Roll Hall of Fame in 1989.

# Ozzy Osbourne

*"I COULDN'T BE A royal. It's like living in a*

*supersonic goldfish bowl."*

(1948-) Born John Michael Osbourne, Ozzy is a heavy metal singer and songwriter who has more recently become known as a television personality. His most famous work has been as the lead singer of Black Sabbath and as a solo artist. Ozzy's style draws from heavy rock and blues, but incorporates dark and eerie lyrics.

*"I GOT RABIES SHOTS for biting the head off a bat, but that's ok – the bat had to get Ozzy shots."*

He has commented that his fans seem to "enjoy being frightened," so he and his band have continued to play on dark themes throughout their career. Between his work with Black Sabbath and his solo work, Ozzy is one of the bestselling artists of all time, with over 100 million records sold worldwide. He has won one Grammy and was inducted into the Rock and Roll Hall of Fame in 2006 with Black Sabbath.

# Page McConnell

*"WE HAVE ENCOURAGED OUR audience,*

*because we avoid the confrontation of regular*

*rock concerts: us up here, you down there.*

*Instead, we're looking for interaction."*

(1963-) Page is a pianist, keyboardist, and
songwriter, best known for being the keyboardist

for Phish. Page is a classically trained pianist and has studied music most of his life. His senior thesis, *The Art of Improvisation*, which he wrote at Goddard College, is still referenced by musicians today. He founded a side project, a jazz-electronica trio called Vida Blue that toured and recorded from 2001-2004. He is proficient in many styles of music and is also a talented vocalist. As such, he is frequently asked to consult and collaborate with other artists.

# Pat Benatar

*"IF AT ANY MOMENT of the day I ever think I'm remotely cool at all, which is hardly ever, I have two daughters who make sure that never happens."*

(1953-) Pat is a singer who rose to fame in the 1980s and with the dawn of MTV and music videos. She is a classically trained vocalist who had plans to attend Julliard, when she suddenly decided a musical career was not what she wanted. A Liza Minelli concert inspired her to change her mind, and she began singing at local clubs. After being discovered by record producers, her rise to popularity was quick. She was the first female artist to appear on MTV. Over the span of her career, she has had 15 Top 40 hits and has won four Grammy awards.

# Patrick Stump

*"NO ONE'S BUSY THINKING bad things about you. They're all too busy thinking bad things about themselves."*

(1984-) Patrick is a singer-songwriter and multi-instrumentalist, best known as the lead singer of Fall Out Boy. Fall Out Boy has been a mainstay of pop and alternative radio stations ever since their 2005 breakout album, *From Under the Cork Tree*. They released two more albums over the next several years, but each one saw declining sales. After taking a nearly three-year hiatus, Fall Out Boy made a huge comeback with an album that debuted at number one. Their sixth album, *American Beauty/American Psycho* is scheduled to be released in January 2015.

*"WHEN YOU HAVE A bad day, a really bad day, try to treat the world better than it treated you."*

# Patti Smith

*"I DON'T THINK PUBLIC life in and of itself*

*can destroy you. I think it's the way people react*

*to it, and some people are more sturdy than*

*others… I don't think any one faction can be*

*blamed for a person's self-destruction – a certain*

*amount of that has to be innate."*

(1946-) Patti is a singer-songwriter who took the punk scene by storm in the 1970s. In addition to her music career, she is also a successful poet, journalist, and author. Many artists, particularly women, have cited Patti as an influence, as she is never afraid to produce music that is raw, authentic, and emotional. Her style often combines spoken word with punk rock accompaniment. She has frequently collaborated with other artists, and she was inducted into the Rock and Roll Hall of Fame in 2007.

# Paul McCartney

*"I USED TO THINK anyone doing anything weird was weird. Now I know that it is people that call others weird that are weird."*

(1942-) Paul is best known as the bassist and one of the founding members of the Beatles. His songwriting partnership with John Lennon was almost as legendary as the Beatles's music itself.

*"THE RUMORS OF MY death have been greatly exaggerated."*

Since the disbanding of the Beatles, Paul has also had a successful solo career, and he has branched out into composing, both in classical and electronic genres. He has written or co-written 32 number one singles, more than any other artist. He has won 18 Grammys and has won the Grammy Lifetime Achievement Award twice: once as a solo artist and once with the Beatles. He was inducted into the Rock and Roll Hall of Fame as a solo artist in 1999.

# Paul Rodgers

*"THERE'S NO SHORTCUT BETWEEN being in*

*your living room and being a rock star. I think*

*you have to go out there and do the gigs, and*

*struggle with the promoters and do the mileage.*

*That separates the people that really want with*

*the ones that say, 'what, we have to drive to*

*Glasgow now, it's four in the fucking morning".*

*That's what you do if you're passionate about it,*

*and you'll have a puncture on the way."*

(1949-) Paul has an unmistakable voice and is best known as the lead singer for Bad Company. He also has performed and recorded with Queen, in addition to having a successful solo career. Bad Company toured extensively in the 1970s, selling out arenas and achieving highly impressive record sales.

*"I MEDITATE DAILY, AND I started way back in '67 when I was 17. I drifted away from it for years but always came back. It's a very good place to be when you want to centre yourself and figure out*

*what's important to you in terms of your next step.*

*There's a tonne of things going on in your mind*

*and you can be very confused and pulled different*

*ways. Very often there's one thing that if you do*

*that it will unlock the door to a lot of other things.*

*Or as someone said, it's better than sitting around*

*doing nothing."*

Paul left the band in 1982, but returned in 1998 after working as a solo artist. He has been highly sought-after as a vocalist and was rumored to have been asked to join the Doors following Jim Morrison's death. As of 2014, he continues to record on his own and collaborate with other artists, and he is reportedly working with Bad Company again.

# Paul Simon

*"IF YOU CAN GET humor and seriousness at the same time, you've created a special little thing, and that's what I'm looking for, because if you get pompous, you lose everything."*

(1941-) Paul is a singer-songwriter, famous for his work in the duo Simon & Garfunkel, and also for his solo work. He wrote most of the songs that he and Art Garfunkel recorded together. His style is mainly acoustic folk rock, and his lyrics reflect either personal experiences or his opinions and beliefs about the world.

He is considered to be one of the best songwriters of this generation and is often cited as an influence by other artists. He has won 12 Grammys and has been inducted into the Rock and Roll Hall of Fame twice: in 1990 as part of Simon & Garfunkel, and in 2001 as a solo artist.

# Paul Stanley

*"WHEN YOU START FOOLING around with drugs, you're hurting your creativity, you're hurting your health. Drugs are death, in one form or another. If they don't kill you, they kill your soul. And if your soul's dead, you've got nothing to offer anyway."*

(1952-) Born Stanley Bert Eisen, Paul is the co-lead singer songwriter for KISS. Despite his rock background, he has also been recognized as a gifted classical singer and has recorded a duet with opera singer Sarah Brightman as well as playing the title role in a Toronto-based production of *Phantom of the Opera.*

*"WHENEVER ANYBODY COMES TO me with a way that I can give something back, it would be ungrateful at this point in my life not to say yes."*

He has worked briefly as a solo artist, but his primary effort has always been with KISS, only missing one show when he was hospitalized with a heart ailment.

*"THE GREAT THING ABOUT rock-n-roll is that you realize the top of the mountain is big enough for more than one band."*

He was born with a deformed ear, affecting both his hearing and his appearance. He currently does work for AboutFace, an organization that helps and supports people with facial abnormalities.

*"CREDIBILITY IS SOMEONE ELSE'S idea of what I should be doing."*

*"DON'T KID YOURSELF. THE guy who's onstage in ripped up jeans is wearing as much a costume as I am."*

# Perry Farrell

*"SOMETIMES TO REALIZE YOU were well,*

*someone must come along and hurt you."*

(1959-) Perry is best known as the lead singer for Jane's Addiction. He also fronted the band Porno for Pyros and is a successful DJ performing under the name DJ Peretz. With Jane's Addiction, he created the now-annual Lollapalooza festival, which showcases alternative, punk, hip-hop, and heavy metal bands.

Jane's Addiction was one of the pioneering bands in the alternative metal movement of the 1990s, and they have influenced bands such as Tool, Korn, and Rage Against the Machine. They have released four studio albums, two of which have been certified Platinum by the RIAA.

*"IF YOU'RE NOT PART of the freaks, you're part of the boredom."*

# Pete Townshend

*"WHEN I GREW UP, what was interesting for me was that music was color and life was gray. So music for me has always been more than entertainment."*

(1945-) Pete is a singer-songwriter and multi-instrumentalist, best known as the lead guitarist and songwriter for The Who. He has never had formal training on any of the instruments he plays, including the guitar, mandolin, ukulele, violin, bass, synthesizer, banjo, accordion, drums, and harmonica.

He is credited with writing over 100 songs for The Who as well as over 100 songs for solo projects and side projects like commercial and radio jingles. He has also achieved success as a writer, having written several books and plays. He frequently appears on lists of the "greatest rock guitarists of all time," and he was inducted into the Rock and Roll Hall of Fame in 1990.

# Peter Buck

*"WE'RE THE ACCEPTABLE EDGE of the*

*unacceptable stuff."*

(1956-) Peter is best known as the lead guitarist for R.E.M., although he has been part of many side projects as well. He plays simple, but powerful chords and makes frequent use of open strings, which creates a distinctive sound and attitude for which R.E.M. has become famous. He has produced albums for many other artists, and has also been working on some solo material.

# Phil Collins

*"BEYOND A CERTAIN POINT, the music isn't*

*mine anymore. It's yours."*

(1951-) Phil is a multi-instrumentalist most

famous for being a drummer. He was the

drummer and lead singer for Genesis and has

since had a successful solo career. He is one of

the best-selling artists of all time, being one of only three artists (the others being Paul McCartney and Michael Jackson) to have sold over 100 million albums both as a solo artist and as a member of a group.

*"YOU KNOW, I'VE RELEASED some great records and I've released some dogs. But frankly, the fun is in creating the thing."*

His trademark synthesized pop sound has drawn a lot of criticism from both critics and other musicians, particularly rock musicians, but while all may not like his style, no one can question his skill or his mass appeal to pop fans. He has won seven Grammy awards and was inducted into the Rock and Roll Hall of Fame in 2010.

*"I'M FASCINATED BY WHAT people will do to each other. Actually, I'm sort of interested in the gory details of life."*

*"YOU KNOW, A SONG is like a kid. You bring it up. And sometimes something you thought was going to be fantastic, by the time it's finished, is a bit of a disappointment."*

# Pink

*"ONCE YOU FIGURE OUT what respect tastes like, it tastes better than attention. But you have to get there."*

(1979-) Born Alecia Beth Moore, Pink is a singer-songwriter who began her career as an R & B singer and has crossed over to mainstream pop. She has a powerful voice with a raspy edge to it that brings a bit of soulful emotion to everything she sings.

She is also known for her acrobatic stage performances, often using aerial equipment as part of her shows. She has a feisty personality and public image that has broken down barriers and helped other powerful vocalists become successful in the pop industry. She has won three Grammy awards, and she has sold over 40 million records worldwide.

# Ray Charles

*"AFFLUENCE SEPARATES PEOPLE.*

*POVERTY knits 'em together."*

(1930-2004) Ray was a singer-songwriter and one of the pioneers of soul music. Like James Brown and Little Richard, Ray fused blues, gospel, jazz, and R & B to create a style that delighted fans of all genres. He also was the first African-American artist to be given full artistic control of his album by a major record label.

His contribution to racial integration of the music industry made him one of the most significant artists of all time. He also became completely blind by age seven, thereby being one of the first artists to not only overcome racial barriers, but also physical ones. He won 12 Grammy awards, in addition to the Grammy Lifetime Achievement Award, and he was inducted into the Rock and Roll Hall of Fame in

1986. His rendition of "Georgia On My Mind" became the official state song of Georgia in 1979.

*"MY VERSION OF 'GEORGIA' became the state song of Georgia. That was a big thing for me, man. It really touched me. Here is a state that used to lynch people like me suddenly declaring my version of a song as its state song. That is touching."*

# Regina Spektor

*"TOMORROW YOU MIGHT GET a phone call about something wonderful and you might get a phone call about something terrible."*

(1980-) Regina is a singer-songwriter known for her eclectic style that incorporates elements of folk, jazz, rock, and indie pop. She began her career in small clubs in New York as part of the

421

anti-folk scene, and she self-published three albums that she sold at her early gigs. Her fourth album included the hit, "Fidelity," which launched her into mainstream popularity. Her songs have since been used in multiple movies and televisions shows, and she was nominated for a Grammy award in 2013.

# Ringo Starr

*"AT THE END OF the day, I can end up just totally wacky, because I've made mountains out of molehills. With meditation, I can keep them as molehills."*

(1940-) Born Richard Starkey Jr., Ringo is best known as the drummer for the Beatles. Ringo is famous for having a more simplistic technique than some of the athletic drummers like Keith Moon or John Bonham, but his sense of musicality is unmatched. Recording engineers and producers give him high praise for always being consistent and for creating drumbeats that are completely distinctive and integral to each individual song.

He plays other instruments in addition to the drums and is a prolific songwriter, too. He contributed lines of lyrics to some of the Beatles's most famous songs. He has released 17 albums as a solo artist.

# Ritchie Blackmore

*"THE ONLY WAY YOU can get good, unless you're a genius, is to copy. That's the best thing. Just steal."*

(1945-) Ritchie is a multi-instrumentalist and songwriter who is best known as one of the original members of Deep Purple. Deep Purple, along with Led Zeppelin and Black Sabbath were one of the early pioneers of hard rock and heavy metal. They took progressive rock to a new level and have influenced some of the biggest names in music like Metallica and Van Halen.

Ritchie stuck with the band through many of their early lineup changes, but eventually left in 1994 to pursue his own projects. Deep Purple has been nominated twice for the Rock and Roll Hall of Fame but has yet to be inducted.

# Rivers Cuomo

*"I DECIDED TO TRY celibacy because I heard it would help the meditation, and I tried meditation because I heard it would help with the music. So, it all really comes back to the music."*

(1970-) Rivers is the lead singer, guitarist, and primary songwriter for Weezer. Weezer exploded on to the alternative rock scene with their debut self-titled album (now known as *The Blue Album*) and its two major singles, "Buddy Holly" and "The Sweater Song." Although their sound has evolved into a much more pop-driven one, they still embody the attitude of alternative rock and are often considered a "mascot" of sorts for the genre.

In addition to his work with Weezer, Rivers has also released several solo works, mostly comprised of raw and discarded material from various Weezer recording sessions.

# Rob Zombie

*"PROBABLY THE BIGGEST THING that surprises people is that I am obsessed with hockey. I grew up in the Boston area, so I am obsessed with hockey since I was a little kid."*

(1965-) Born Robert Bartleh Cummings, Rob is a singer-songwriter and has more recently forged a successful career in the film industry, both as a writer and as a director/producer.

*"ONCE YOU FEEL LIKE you're being dictated by other people's expectations, it usually backfires."*

As a musician, he is known for founding the band White Zombie in addition to having a prolific solo career. His style incorporates elements of heavy metal and shock rock, with his lyrics often center around horror and sci-fi themes.

*"GREAT THINGS COME OUT of being hungry and cold. Once you're pampered, you get lazy."*

*"MY ADVICE: DON'T QUIT. When I got to New York City, I lived so far below the poverty line, because I didn't give in and get a job at 7-Eleven. I think you can thrive in misery."*

# Robert Plant

*"WHENEVER I HAVE BID a hasty goodbye to a loved one, I have always made sure that my record collection was safely stored away in the boot of the car."*

(1948-) Robert is a singer-songwriter best known as the lead singer and songwriter for Led

Zeppelin. His vocal range is impressive and has inspired many other famous vocalists like Freddie Mercury, Geddy Lee, and Axl Rose. Since the disbanding of Led Zeppelin, Robert has gone on to be part of many musical projects, most recently adopting more of a folk/blues sound, which is in contrast to his wild rock performances from the Zeppelin years.

*"YOU CAN'T GIVE UP something you really believe in for financial reasons. If you die by the roadside – so be it. But at least you know you've tried. Ten minutes in the music scene was the equal of one hundred years outside of it."*

His collaboration with country and folk singer Alison Krauss in 2008 won six Grammy awards, and he currently tours with his band, the Sensational Space Shifters. Led Zeppelin was inducted into the Rock and Roll Hall of Fame in 1995.

*"I THINK LED ZEPPELIN must have worn some of the most peculiar clothing that men had ever been seen to wear without cracking a smile."*

# Robin Zander

*"WE'RE FROM ROCKFORD, ILLINOIS, but*

*we've always thought international."*

(1953-) Robin is the lead singer for Cheap Trick. They started out as a humble band from the Midwest who played a lot of local gigs but were not being noticed on a national level. Although they were not gaining fame in the United States, they had a rabid fan base in Japan, and it was their success overseas that would eventually make them chart-toppers at home. They have truly made their career on the road, with almost 40 years of non-stop touring. They have influenced many bands, and they continue to collaborate with and tour alongside other musical acts.

# Roger Daltrey

*"NO, I WAS TWO years older than the other*

*guys. I was a war baby. My family were a lot*

*poorer than they were. I'd had to fight too hard*

*for anything I had in my life and to smash things*

*up for me."*

(1944-) Roger is the lead singer for The Who.

His musical relationship with guitarist and

songwriter Pete Townshend is an unusual one in that Pete writes the lyrics, while Roger becomes the medium through which they are expressed. Roger's voice has become one of the most recognizable ones in rock music, and his charismatic stage presence is one of the defining characteristics of The Who.

*"FIRST OF ALL, YOU have to understand that I'm like anybody else. When I hear my voice on a record, I absolutely loathe my voice. I cannot stand my voice."*

He also has released eight solo albums and has collaborated with many other artists. Along with the rest of The Who, Roger received a Grammy Lifetime Achievement Award in 2001.

# Roger Waters

*I'M IN COMPETITION WITH myself, and I'm*

*losing.*

(1943-) Roger is best known as the bassist, lyricist, co-lead signer, and conceptual director of Pink Floyd, one of the most commercially successful bands of all time. Their progressive style and intellectual lyrics lent themselves easily to concept albums like *Dark Side of the Moon, Animals,* and *The Wall.*

Roger and co-lead singer David Gilmour have become famous for feuding over creative control and intellectual property rights, and it is only in recent years that they agreed to appear together after almost 20 years of separation. Pink Floyd has sold over 250 million records worldwide and they are cited as an influence by almost every rock band that has ever existed. They were inducted into the Rock and Roll Hall of Fame in 1996.

# Ronnie James Dio

*"THE SPACE SHUTTLE JUST flew over the Niji*

*Offices in Burbank! God bless America!"*

(1942-2010) Ronnie was best known as the

lead vocalist for Black Sabbath, his eponymous

442

band Dio, and several other heavy metal bands. His only musical training came from learning to play the trumpet at a young age, during which he learned proper breathing technique.

During his career, he attributed his powerful singing ability to this training. He was revered by fans and critics for his voice and by his peers for being a man of integrity and substance. He sold over 47 million albums worldwide.

# Ronnie Wood

*"WHEN I'M LEFT ON my own I'm my own worst enemy."*

(1947-) Ronnie is a guitarist best known for his role as a member of the Rolling Stones. He also does a lot of solo projects and owns his own record company. He focuses mainly on slide guitar, but has also been known to play rhythm guitar and bass, depending on the song and whom he is working with. He has been inducted into the Rock and Roll Hall of Fame twice: with the Rolling Stones in 1989 and with the Faces in 2012.

# Roy Orbison

*"I MAY BE A living legend, but that sure don't*

*help when I've got to change a flat tire."*

(1936-1988) Roy was a singer-songwriter known for his distinctive low, sultry voice, and his emotional ballads. His voice was often described as "other-worldly," as it was completely different from anything else that was being played on the radio at the time. He never conformed to popular conventions of style in either his appearance or his music, and although this made him somewhat of a man of mystery, it also made him all the more popular. He received six Grammy awards, including the Grammy Lifetime Achievement Award, and he was inducted into the Rock and Roll Hall of Fame in 1987.

# Scott Stapp

*"I WAS RAISED IN a climate where I believed in God because I was afraid of going to hell – and I didn't think that was the right way to fall in love with somebody."*

(1973-) Scott is a singer-songwriter best known as the former lead singer for Creed. Since the breakup of Creed, he has also released two solo albums. Creed was hugely successful in the late 1990s and early 2000s as part of the post-grunge movement, and their second album, *Human Clay*, was certified Diamond by the RIAA.

# Sebastian Bach

*"IF I EVER GROW up, I don't want to be around*

*for it."*

(1968-) Sebastian is the former lead singer of Skid Row and has more recently also forged a career in acting. Skid Row rose to fame with the help of fellow New Jersey band, Bon Jovi. Their first two albums are both multi-platinum hits. After leaving Skid Row, Sebastian went on to concentrate on solo work in addition to performing in theater and with other musicians. He has frequently appeared on television as a reality show personality and in character roles.

# Shannon Hoon

*"ARE YOU FRUSTRATED BECAUSE of the way*

*people perceive you, or are you happy enough*

*about the things you've realized that you can*

*tolerate the way people perceive you?"*

(1967-1995) Shannon was the lead singer of

Blind Melon. Through a friendship with Axl

Rose, Blind Melon was able to showcase their unique alternative style to record companies, eventually being signed by Capitol Records. Their single, "No Rain," from their first album, gained international recognition thanks to the creative music video that became a huge hit on MTV. They were in the middle of a tour supporting their second album, when Shannon died of a cocaine overdose at the age of 28.

# Shannon Leto

*"USE YOUR IMAGINATION NOT to scare yourself to death, but inspire you to live."*

(1970-) Shannon is the drummer for 30 Seconds to Mars, a band that he started with his younger brother, Jared. Shannon is known for energetic stage performances and for his aptitude for mixing traditional acoustic drumming with electronic and experimental sounds. He has also experimented with acting, appearing in several television shows and films with his brother and a few on his own. 30 Seconds to Mars has sold over 10 million albums worldwide.

# Shaun Morgan

*"INSECURITY KILLS all that is beautiful."*

(1978-) Shaun is the lead singer for Seether. They have achieved huge mainstream success, with three of their albums reaching Gold status and one becoming certified Platinum. Their style is noticeably influenced by heavy and alternative bands of the early 1990s, such as Nirvana, Nine

Inch Nails, and Korn. Their songs have been part of multiple soundtracks for both television shows and video games. Their sixth studio album was released in 2014.

# Sheena Easton

*"WE ARE SUPPOSED TO enjoy the good stuff now, while we can, with the people we love. Life has a funny way of teaching us that lesson over and over again."*

(1959-) Sheena is a singer, recording artist, and actress whose talent was discovered in 1979 on the first reality television show, a British show called *The Big Time*. She has gone on to record 16 studio albums and perform collaborations with some of the most popular artists of all time, including Prince, Kenny Rogers, and Babyface. She has won two Grammy awards and has sold over 20 million records worldwide.

# Shirley Manson

*"I AM NOT A sexy woman, I'm not beautiful, I'm not a sex kitten, I don't flirt with people, yet I've been tagged more of a sex symbol than women who truly are, and I think that's solely because I don't reveal too much: people are curious."*

(1966-) Shirley is a singer-songwriter best known as the lead singer for alternative rock band Garbage. She also has a successful acting career. Her distinctive voice and strong personality have made her an inspirational and influential figure for many female artists.

She is proof that even talented and charismatic performers face setbacks—her first audition for Garbage did not earn her a spot in the band. She was given another chance after some time, and not only did they bring her on board, but she also quickly became the face of the band and one of their principal songwriters. During Garbage's hiatuses, she has worked on solo material and collaborated with other artists. Garbage has sold over 12 million records worldwide.

# Sid Vicious

*"YOU CAN'T ARREST ME, I'm a rockstar."*

(1957-1979) Born John Simon Ritchie, Sid was best known as the bassist for the Sex Pistols. Sid was said to have had the right attitude for punk, which fit with the Sex Pistols's image perfectly, but that he didn't have much technical skill, especially with the bass.

*"WE ARE BETTER THAN anyone, ain't we?*

*Except for the Eagles, the Eagles are better than*

*us."*

Guitarist Steve Jones helped him learn and even stepped in to cover him during early recordings, but no one could deny Sid's stage presence as a major factor of the Sex Pistols's popularity. He became infamous for reckless behavior, drug use, and eventually stabbing and killing his girlfriend, Nancy Spungen. Less than four months later, he died of a drug overdose at the age of 21.

# Slash

*"I HAD NO ASPIRATIONS to be a musician, but I picked up a guitar for two seconds and haven't put it down since."*

(1965-) Born Saul Hudson, Slash is the guitarist for Guns 'n Roses and for the supergroup Velvet Revolver. His signature sound and catchy guitar riffs are unmistakable to anyone familiar with rock music.

*"I NEVER WANT TO draw attention to myself,*

*but that's all I do."*

Although Slash eventually left Guns 'n Roses due to his tumultuous relationship with lead singer Axl Rose, they were extremely successful as a band, having sold over 100 million records worldwide. They are also credited with completing the longest rock tour in history, which was 28 months long. He is currently focusing on his solo career and released his third solo album in 2014.

# Smokey Robinson

*"THAT'S BECAUSE WE DID not set out to make*

*black music. We set out to make quality music*

*that everyone could enjoy and listen to."*

(1940-) Born William Robinson Jr., Smokey is an R & B singer-songwriter who is most famous for founding and fronting The Miracles. With The Miracles, Smokey wrote and performed 26 Top 40 hits, and he has also had several hits as a solo artist. In addition to writing songs for himself and his group, he has also written and produced for other top acts such as Marvin Gaye, The Temptations, and the Marvelettes. He was inducted into the Rock and Roll Hall of Fame in 1987.

# Stephan Jenkins

*"MY MUSIC IS MY way to rearrange the world*

*according to my own hopes."*

(1964-) Stephan is the lead singer, guitarist, and primary songwriter for Third Eye Blind. Third Eye Blind began their career as an opening act for Oasis, but they had such a dynamic and impressive set, they were often asked back onstage for an encore—incredibly rare for an opening band. Their first album went six times platinum in the United States, and quite a few singles from that album are still frequently played on the radio. They have sold 12 million albums worldwide.

# Steve Morse

*"THE IRONY IS WHEN people say they want to do something and then don't do it. I don't understand."*

(1954-) Steve is a guitarist who founded the Dixie Dregs and has been the guitarist for Deep Purple since 1994. He is also a successful solo artist. His style combines multiple genres, including rock, jazz, blues, funk, country, and classical. He has a natural gift for composing, which has helped his guitar technique as well as his ability to improvise during performances. He is often cited as an influence and frequently appears near the top of "best guitarist" lists.

# Steve Vai

*"I DON'T BELIEVE IN 'greatest,' I believe in favorites."*

(1960-) Steve is a guitarist, songwriter, composer, and producer who is known for his solo work and his collaborations with various artists. He has recorded and toured with numerous acts, including Whitesnake, David Lee Roth, and Public Image Ltd. He is considered to be one of the most technically advanced guitarists in rock music and is known for his use of floating vibrato and complicated rhythms.

Steve is an avid beekeeper and sells honey for his charitable foundation. He has sold over 15 million albums and has won three Grammy awards.

# Steven Van Zandt

*"YOUNG FANS WANT TO know about the past and older fans also want to find new music."*

(1950-) Steven is a musician, actor, and radio personality. In the music industry, he is best known as the guitarist and mandolin player for Bruce Springsteen's E Street Band. He also has produced and written songs for numerous other artists. While they were primarily Bruce Springsteen's backing band, the talent of the E Street band members is well-known in the music business, and some or all of them have recorded, and toured with other musicians. As part of the E Street Band, Steven was inducted into the Rock and Roll Hall of Fame in 2014.

# Stevie Nicks

*"EVEN IN MY REALLY bad, drugged-out days, I didn't go away. I still toured, still did interviews. I never gave up the fight. That's why I'm who I am today, because I didn't leave. And I think I made the right choice."*

(1948-) Stevie is a singer-songwriter who is famous for being the lead singer of Fleetwood Mac as well as for having a successful solo career. Her lyrics are often symbolic and derived from personal experiences or her reactions to things she encounters like literature and nature.

*"IF YOU HAVE STAGE fright, it never goes away. But then I wonder: is the key to that magical performance because of the fear?"*

Her strong, distinctive voice, along with her bohemian fashion sense has made her an icon for women, particularly in the music industry. Countless female artists cite her as an influence or an inspiration. She was inducted into the Rock

and Roll Hall of Fame in 1998.

# Stevie Ray Vaughan

*"YOU SEE, WE ARE here, as far as I can tell, to*

*help each other; our brothers, our sisters, our*

*friends, our enemies. That is to help each other*

*and not hurt each other."*

(1954-1990) Stevie was a singer-songwriter and record producer, most notable for his signature blues-rock style. In his short career, he released six studio albums and six live albums, and became the face of electric blues. He was heavily influenced by Jimi Hendrix and wanted to continue the legacy that had been left after Jimi's death.

*"I ACTUALLY WANTED TO be a drummer, but I didn't have any drums."*

Although he struggled with drugs and alcohol, Stevie became sober in 1986 and was committed to helping others do the same. His tragic death at the age of 35 in a helicopter accident was a huge loss for the music industry as well as for the community at large. He won six Grammy awards during his career.

# Syd Barrett

*"I THINK IT'S GOOD if a song has more than one meaning. Maybe that kind of song can reach far more people."*

(1946-2006) Born Roger Keith Barrett, Syd was one of the founding members of Pink Floyd and was the band's original lead singer and primary songwriter. He was experimental in both his musical style and with his lyrics, which gave Pink Floyd their initial distinctive niche in rock music.

*"I DON'T THINK I'M easy to talk about. I've got a very irregular head. And I'm not anything that you think I am anyway."*

As time went on, Syd's behavior become strange and problematic, mostly likely due to mental illness brought on by heavy psychedelic drug use. He was eventually replaced in the band by David Gilmour. He went on to record two solo albums, but then left the public eye.

*"I'M FULL OF DUST and guitars."*

# Taylor Momsen

*"I GET TOLD ALL the time that I'm a fashion icon now, but I don't really know what that means. I just get dressed."*

(1993-) Taylor is the lead singer of The Pretty Reckless, and she is also a model and actress. Taylor's band has played on the Warped Tour as well as in support of other artists such as Evanescence and Marilyn Manson. They have released two studio albums, and their 2014 single, "Heaven Knows," became a number one Billboard hit.

# Ted Nugent

*"DO YOU WANT TO feel good or do you want to*

*do good?"*

(1948-) Ted is a singer-songwriter known for his outspoken political views and his relentless, high-energy touring schedule. He has toured every year since 1967 and has averaged over 300 shows per year.

*"I THINK YOU SHOULD ride the line between fatigue and chaos. The chaos keeps the energy level and spontaneity maximized, while fatigue is just over the edge, and you should try to avoid it."*

He has recorded 14 studio albums, four of which have gone platinum or multi-platinum. He is an adamant supporter of gun ownership rights and the Republican Party. He has appeared on numerous television shows both as himself and in character.

*"VEGETARIANS ARE COOL. ALL I eat are vegetarians – except for the occasional mountain lion steak."*

# Terry Kath

*"SOMETIMES I'LL BE PLAYING along and find*

*I'm missing the strings. I'll worry about it for*

*days until I notice that the pick has worn down to*

*half its size."*

(1946-1978) Terry was a founding member of Chicago, and he was their original lead singer and guitarist. He was considered to be a huge musical talent, both for his technical ability on the guitar and also for his ear for composing.

Chicago was an unusual band in that they had horns and saxophones in addition to typical rock instruments. Terry combined all of the instruments seamlessly in the songs he wrote. Many musicians and rock critics believe that Terry was one of the most underrated musicians and bandleaders of all time, mainly due to the fact that Chicago always presented themselves as a unit rather than as a band with a clear front man.

Terry's death of an accidental gunshot wound to the head at the age of 31 was one of the music industry's biggest losses.

# Thom Yorke

*"I GREW UP BELIEVING that I was*

*fundamentally powerless."*

(1968-) Thom is the lead singer and primary songwriter for Radiohead and supergroup Atoms for Peace. He is a multi-instrumentalist, although he generally prefers to play the guitar in performances. He has an ethereal and angelic voice, which is emphasized by his heavy use of falsetto.

*"I KNOW I'M PARANOID and neurotic. I've*

*made a career out of it. "*

His style has become more experimental over the years as he has branched out into electronic-driven music. He has sold over 30 million records worldwide and is frequently considered to be one of the greatest singers in rock music.

*"BEING IN A BAND turns you into a child and*

*keeps you there. "*

~

*"THE PEOPLE IN CHARGE, globally, are maniacs. They are maniacs, and unless we do something about it, these people are going to deprive us of a future."*

# Tina Turner

*"I BELIEVE THAT IF you'll just stand up and go, life will open up for you."*

(1939-) Born Anna Mae Bullock, Tina is a singer, dancer, and actress. She is known for being a powerful vocalist and for maintaining high-energy on stage while dancing and singing at the same time. She began her musical career when she married Ike Turner and became one-half of the duo Ike & Tina Turner. After Ike's substance abuse problem led to a decline in musical ability and domestic violence, Tina struck out on her own.

She initially struggled as a solo artist, but with the help of her fan base and industry friends, she became hugely successful. She has won 11 Grammy awards, including three Grammy Hall of Fame Awards. She was inducted into the Rock and Roll Hall of Fame in 1991.

# Tina Weymouth

*"SOMETIMES, YOU HAVE TO go through a*

*phase, whether you like it or not."*

(1950-) Tina is currently the bassist for Tom Tom Club, but is best known as a founding member and the bassist for the new wave rock band, Talking Heads. Talking Heads created a style that fused rock with elements of post-punk, grunge, and avant-garde experimental dance music. They were a huge success in the 1980s, and seemed to quit just as they had skyrocketed to the height of their popularity. Despite lead singer David Byrne's lack of interest in continuing as a band, Tina and her husband, Talking Heads drummer Chris Frantz, forged on and formed Tom Tom Club.

# Tom DeLonge

*"IT'S ACTUALLY COOL TO be positive and optimistic and idealistic. It's cool to see yourself doing beautiful, great things."*

(1975-) Tom is a guitarist and songwriter, most famous for being the lead singer of Blink-182 and Angels & Airwaves. He was an avid skateboarder as a kid and had always wanted to be in a band, which became a dream he simply refused to let go of.

He learned how to play guitar in high school, where he met Blink-182 bassist Mark Hoppus. They started out as a punk band, but gradually shifted more into punk-pop as they became more commercially successful. Tom started Angels & Airwaves as a multi-media side project after Blink-182 went on hiatus in 2004. Blink-182 has since reunited to record and tour, and they have sold over 35 million albums worldwide.

# Tom Morello

*"MUSIC, I THINK, IS best when it honestly explores personal demons, and it stirs around in the silt of the psyche to find out what's really there."*

(1964-) Tom is a musician who first became famous as the lead guitarist for Rage Against the Machine. He has since participated in numerous musical projects including Audioslave, The Nightwatchman, and Street Sweeper Social Club. Currently, he is also touring as part of Bruce Springsteen's E Street Band.

His guitar style is unique, and he has invented several techniques that make his instruments sound like "anything but a guitar." He, like his Rage Against the Machine band mates, is an outspoken political activist. He formed the Axis of Justice, along with System of a Down front man Serj Tankian, which is a non-profit organization dedicated to bring musicians and fans together to fight for social justice.

# Tom Petty

*"MOST THINGS I WORRY about never happen anyway."*

(1950-) Tom is a multi-instrumentalist, singer, songwriter, and record producer, best known as the lead singer of Tom Petty & The Heartbreakers. He also was part of the supergroup

Traveling Wilburys and has had a successful solo career. His style is mostly traditional rock or blues-rock, and his songs have a pop appeal that reaches a wide audience. He still tours, and he released an album that debuted at number one on the Billboard 200 in 2014. He has sold over 80 million records worldwide and was inducted into the Rock and Roll Hall of Fame in 2002.

# Tommy Iommi

*"I WAS MOSTLY SURPRISED by the rap artists, actually, that were influenced by Sabbath. That was a surprise. But it's very nice and I'm very honored. It's nice to know after 27 years now that what I said in the first place has stuck, and that was the belief in it."*

(1948-) Tommy is the lead guitarist and primary songwriter for Black Sabbath. He is widely considered to be the creator of heavy metal, as he was the first guitarist to ever produce that heavy, industrial sound.

His signature sound was born out of a factory accident, in which he lost the tips of two of his fingers. As a result, he detuned his guitar to make it easier to play, and bassist Geezer Butler did the same to match him. This detuning created darker and creepier-sounding melodies, something that caught on with other heavy metal bands. He has recorded three solo albums and has been part of many collaborations.

# Tommy Lee

*"I'M A REALLY COOL, mellow guy. I'm not as crazy as everybody thinks."*

(1962-) Tommy is best known as the drummer for Mötley Crüe, but he also has had a solo career and is a popular DJ for festivals and clubs. He is famous for his wild stage presence, including his famous floating and spinning drum kit, and for doing outrageous things like mooning the audience.

*"IT'S ALWAYS INTERESTING TO me that we all hear music differently. It's an awesome experience to hear what other people hear."*

In addition to his musical pursuits, Tommy has also been on several reality television shows, and he is a prominent activist for animal rights and PETA.

*"I DON'T THINK ANYBODY should ever touch anybody in anger, ever."*

# Tommy Shaw

*"SUCCESS IS FICKLE BUT creativity is a gift."*

(1953-) Tommy is a singer-songwriter, most famous for being a guitarist and lead singer for Styx. He was not an original member of the band, but was brought on in 1976 to replace John Curulewski who had suddenly decided to leave the band right before they were about to go on a national tour. Tommy and keyboardist Dennis DeYoung traded songwriting duties, but had different and opposing styles. Tommy eventually left Styx to pursue a solo career because he didn't like the pop and theatrical direction in which the band was headed. Styx was the first band to have four consecutive multi-platinum albums, three of which were triple-platinum.

*"I WISH I HAD a nickel for every song that I've left in the bathroom, written down on a matchbox, or just totally forgotten about."*

# Tori Amos

*"I HAVE SO MANY different personalities in me,*

*and I still feel lonely."*

(1963-) Born Myra Ellen Amos, Tori is a singer-songwriter and pianist. She was a child prodigy and was accepted to the Johns Hopkins Peabody Institute of Music when she was only five years old.

*"I KNOW I'M AN acquired taste – I'm anchovies. And not everybody wants those hairy little things."*

She explores personal and feminist topics through her lyrics, and she is one of few alternative rock artists to primarily use a piano instead of a guitar. She has sold over 12 million albums worldwide.

*"I'M A CONDUIT FOR telling people's stories.*

*It's a privilege."*

# Tré Cool

*"SCHOOL IS PRACTICE FOR the future, and practice makes perfect and nobody's perfect so why bother."*

(1972-) Born Frank Edwin Wright III, Tré Cool is the drummer for Green Day. He has a unique drumming style and an athletic stage presence, which have earned him comparisons to both John Bonham and Keith Moon. Even the other members of Green Day have said that it takes time and patience to play cohesively with someone as creative and unpredictable as Tré.

# Trent Reznor

*"I REALIZED THAT I was afraid to really, really try something, 100%, because I had never reached true failure."*

(1965-) Trent is a singer-songwriter and record producer. He is the creative force behind Nine Inch Nails, and he has recently gained fame for his film scores, specifically *The Social Network*, *The Girl With the Dragon Tattoo*, and *Gone Girl*. He is the only official member of Nine Inch Nails and frequently changes his touring lineup to reflect changes in the overall styles and moods of his songs. He has won two Grammy awards in 13 nominations and has sold over 20 million records worldwide.

# Trey Anastasio

*"WHAT I THOUGHT AT the moment was the worst thing that could happen was absolutely the biggest gift I've received."*

(1964-) Trey is the guitarist and main lead singer for Phish. He also has had a successful solo career and has collaborated with other rock artists and orchestras. He is credited with many of the concepts that serve as the basis for Phish's music, through-composition, improvisation, and lyrics that often come from his own writings or that of longtime friend and writing partner, Tom Marshall.

Being classically trained and having studied music at the collegiate level, Trey is an accomplished technical player and has a unique sound that he has cultivated over many years. In 2013, he won a Tony award for his score to *Hands on a Hardbody*.

# Van Morrison

*"MUSIC IS SPIRITUAL. The music business is*

*not."*

(1945-) Van is a singer-songwriter whose
style ranges from blues to R & B to traditional,
almost hymnal music. His early hit single,

"Brown Eyed Girl," is still one of the most-requested songs by DJs around the world, and much of his music has influenced other artists.

*"SINGING IS MY PROFESSION – there is no*

*plan B."*

He has never been one to cater to the industry and has always preferred to do things his own way. He self-produced his album *Moondance*, which is now widely regarded as one of the best rock albums ever made. Van has won six Grammy awards and was inducted into the Rock and Roll Hall of Fame in 1993.

# Wes Borland

*"THERE MAY BE SOMETHING good in silence.*

*It's a brand new thing. You can hear the funniest*

*little discussions, if you keep turning the volume*

*down. Shut yourself up, and listen out loud."*

(1975-) Wes is most famous for being the guitarist in Limp Bizkit, but is now focused on fronting Black Light Burns. He often performs in body paint or in costume, almost always wearing his custom-made black contact lenses. His guitar style is unique, often using both hands to create patterns—one hand plucks while the other strums chords. He uses primarily seven-string guitars and is frequently cited as one of the best rock and heavy metal guitarists of modern times.

# Zack de la Rocha

*"ONE OF THE GREAT things about young people is that they do question, that they do care deeply about justice, and that they have open minds."*

(1970-) Zack is a rapper and poet best known for fronting Rage Against the Machine. He is an outspoken political activist and often used songwriting as a means for delivering his message. Rage Against the Machine was the most politically charged band to ever have such a mainstream following, and their shows were very polarizing—people either loved or hated them. Following the band's breakup in 2000, Zack collaborated with some other artists and also released a solo album.

*"YOUR ANGER is a gift."*

# Phew!

OH WHAT GOES into a book! And you'd think just picking out *rock star quotes* would be easy! We've written a *lot* of books, just most have been for other people, as ghostwriters. But this was special, and exciting. After the year it took for us to get all of this carefully chosen material together, write bios that follow a certain formula, and so on, we were still surprised at the time needed for editing it into shape and layout that was *just right.*

As we moved things around and formatted, it's not that we created any kind of work of art that others would be blown away by, but that the task became kind of a religious experience *for us.*

That picture of Ace Frehley had to be just right; deciding on how to present the quotes, deciding on how to break things up—it all became obvious to us how sacred we seem to hold certain rock stars. They represent parts of us and our lives.

In general, we're not particularly star-struck or envious of celebrities; it's just they've been the purveyors of music and poetry—things that have always been there for us. Music has never failed to offer something new, sooner or later encapsulating some life aspect or chapter. First cars. First loves. Starting school. Leaving school. Moving. Breakups. Celebrations. Tragedies. Every life moment, happy, sad, or otherwise, dances along to a carefully selected soundtrack.

We couldn't have written this book without each and every one of the rock stars mentioned in it... of course. There is a reason they're stars, and each one of them has spoken to us on a deep level. Thank you to all of you—for your work and your words. For the departed, this is a memorial of sorts, and for those who are still with us, may you continue to inspire your audiences for years to come.

We really love this book. It was so exciting to make—as we did the final edit and it started to take on a life of its own we realized that we each wanted to *read* it! What a great sign! It's a book we are excited about having on our nightstands and desks, and proud to give to close friends, whom we hope will see much more than us, even—not-so-subtly proving we did what we set out to do with this book.

And since this is an acknowledgments opportunity, in another sense Dawn, Fallon, and Luke are our own personal rock stars, as are so many others who have supported and encouraged us.

Hey, it'd be great if this sells, but regardless, we love it, and we're grateful to so many!

You guys rock!

# Bimini Books

We hope you enjoyed our first collection of rock star quotes and hope you'll help us make another one! We invite you to contact us and give us your suggestions.

At Bimini, we are always working to bring you engaging, light, fun and informative books. More are added all the time. To find out about the latest releases and events, please visit Bimini Books online!

www.BiminiBooks.com

# Your Honest Opinion

And as you may know, about the greatest gift you can give a writer (besides buying his or her book of course) is leaving an honest, useful review on Amazon.

*Thanks in advance!*

# About the Authors

## Alison Taylor

HOW MANY TIMES have you heard about something and thought, "I've always wanted to learn more about that," but you just don't have enough time to put in the research?

Alison has had that feeling all too often. After ghostwriting dozens of books on topics ranging from personal finance to starting a new business to anti-aging secrets, she realized that it was time for her to start sharing her own knowledge and experience, too. Alison likes to take life by the handlebars and dive head-first into learning all she can about anything and everything. Her goal is to get people excited about the world around them and to create enthusiasts of all kinds.

She likes to think of herself as a connoisseur of music and, believe it or not, still makes mix tapes for people. Contact Alison at www.BiminiBooks.com to find out what she's listening to right now or if there's a topic you'd really like to see her tackle in a future book.

# Rodney Miles

RODNEY IS THE author of over 50 works of fiction and non-fiction as a ghostwriter, and of over just as many as founder and CEO of Rodney Sanger and Associates (www.Rodney-Sanger.com), a Florida-based ghostwriting and self-publishing assistance firm. Rodney is also a founding partner and CEO of Bimini Books (www.BiminiBooks.com), bringing you enjoyable lifestyle titles to escape and enjoy with.

He lives in Palm Bay, Florida, with his wife of 20 years, beautiful daughter, Fallon, 16 now (believe it or not!), a Saint Bernard and two Pekingese (not by choice), two cats, and an unknown number of bearded dragons of Fallon's, one of which she likes to leave in the bathroom loose without telling me. Acting like a rock star already : )

# List of Rock Stars

Made in the USA
San Bernardino, CA
30 December 2015